The Big Supposer

Lawrence Durrell

The Big Supposer

Lawrence Durrell
A Dialogue with Marc Alyn

**Translated from the French
by Francine Barker**

**Illustrated with paintings
by Lawrence Durrell**

Grove Press, Inc.
New York

Contents

Durrell's Way 7

The River Surveyed 13

The English Death 21

Corfu, the Rectangle and the Circle 35

The Black Book, the War 43

Egypt and the First Movement of the *Quartet* 57

Winged Heels 69

Life in Sommières 79

Poetry: A Tragic Game 87

The Novel Versus Suicide 95

Talking About Writers 105

Elegy on Romanticism and the Closing of the French Brothels 115

Tunc, Nunquam: The Struggle for Happiness 133

Les Suppositoires Requisitoires — Lawrence Durrell 139

Astrological Portrait of Lawrence Durrell by Conrad Moricand 151

Durrell's Way

Uzès to Sommières is not more than about thirty miles across the *garrigue*, which rises in deep green tiers against the blue of the sky on either side of a winding road, dotted here and there with wines, like musical staves or lines of some indecipherable handwriting.

For years I have secretly called this road the Durrell Road, not only because it links my own adopted Languedoc town with the great novelist's, but also because in my mind it has become somehow identified with Durrell's own work: bends, dangerous crossroads, vast open spaces, sun, mistral, the bridge at Dions ('liable to flood') that crosses a silvery river which, depending on the time of year, reveals its bed of hard, dry stones, like Irish oaths, or overflows, ripping up trees and banks with a frenzy that can abate in a matter of minutes.

Around Uzès the *garrigue* is like a line of Racine: a stony harshness, white-hot under the summer sun; but after Dions the view opens out, softly rounded slopes replace the jagged edges which tore the sky where they met. The dominant greens remain in the immediate landscape, but on the horizon, first the hills and then the mountains take on a bluer and bluer hue. Sommières nestles over there in a hollow in the blue.

The road follows the Vidourle, lined with café terraces where the pastis flows free as the river, occasionally sweeping all before it; cross the Roman bridge, built by Tiberius, and follow the road to Durrell's strange house, the only one with a slate roof in a region dominated by the rounded tile.

The house stands between a cemetery and a football pitch, a setting that perfectly symbolizes this mind which oscillates ceaselessly between the metaphysical serious-ness of *The Book of the Dead* and the pleasures of the body. Behind the boundary wall is a tangle of trees and shrubs and then the large, dark, heavy house, which is so surprisingly warm in winter and cool in summer, with its conservatory apparently modelled on the verandah of the family house in Darjeeling, at the foot of the Hima-layas, where Durrell was born. You enter the large, tiled hall on the ground floor through a passage curiously furnished with a butcher's marble-topped table, on which stands the gilded, plaster bust of a man in a wig, of aristocratic countenance (Lavoisier, Laclos?), on wet days to be seen wearing a large hat. Beside the armless statue lies a toy gun loaded with a rubber-tipped arrow —black and red.

Once inside the door you will find something more like a stage set than a room for living in. There is nothing untidy about it, apart from a heap of newly-arrived books, reviews and records lying on a table by the win-dow, waiting to know whether they will be read or listened to, or put away in some dark cupboard. A highly-polished piano slumbers—keys locked—beside a bookcase made of fire bricks and sheets of plate-glass; unreadable, old, *Encyclopaedia Britannica*-type books lean heavily on these fragile shelves as if to demonstrate the tenuity of the fate of culture. . . . Deep, comfortable arm-chairs are arranged in a semi-circle round the fire where scented logs burn from autumn on, their heat inflating the paintings, Epfs-Durrells, and turning the flickering arms of a musical mobile which hangs in one corner.

It was in this setting that the conversations that follow

took place in 1970 and 1971, though I must just make clear that the moment Lawrence Durrell enters, the surroundings seem to disappear: he draws all attention to himself, his very presence obliterating everything else, standing like a screen between the visitor and the furniture.

'I have told you that I was born many.' The quotation, used by the author of *The Black Book* to describe Miller's multi-faceted character, applies equally well to himself. In this one man is contained a host of characters, who take it in turn to answer in his name, to shuffle the cards of the dialogue and the features of his ever-changing face. Behind this positively baroque wardrobe of masks, Durrell's real face remains inaccessible. Pull at a mask and you will find to your amazement that it sticks to the skin; transitory as it may seem, it is, after all, a real face.

Here is a recluse who loves being surrounded by people; a hedonist whose great pleasure is asceticism; a lazy man who never stops working; a man who finds joy in despair; a traveller who enjoys nothing more than quiet contemplation; a dandy truly at his ease in the company of tramps and vagrants; a novelist whose major preoccupation is poetry; an enemy of literature who gives the best of himself to his work.

You must picture all these conflicting elements together in one man, whose physical appearance also changes from minute to minute: his face lighting up or freezing depending on the question, transformed by tiredness from extreme youth to wrinkles, from exuberance to dejected, stony silence; friendly, but with a certain reserve; apparently open, and yet never letting you anywhere near the vast, hidden areas that you sense inside him; instinctively establishing a no-go area between himself and others, only to regret the distance later and to try by some gesture of real warmth to bridge it. But above all he is always on the move, incapable of

11

keeping still, moving his hands as he talks like a fowler or a card-sharper, jumping up to pick out a tune on the piano, put on a record, demonstrate a dance-step between the chairs, and particularly to pour endless glasses of gin. He comes and he goes and he talks without a break, up and down like a jack-in-the-box between the glazed walls of the conservatory, irresistibly reminiscent, with its plants and coloured glass, of an aquarium, gestating new forms of life, hybrids of monsters and angels.

Eagerly questioning Lawrence Durrell about his life and his work, I struggled hard not to yield to the fascination—a very real fascination—that this extraordinary man exerts over all who come near him. I get the impression that here and there I succeeded. The attentive reader will find answers in the places where he shies off or refuses to comment. The important thing is to watch, sometimes, on the surface of words and silences, the darting phosphorescence of a gaze, turned from the deep, to dance over things, people and ideas like the blue flame across a bowl of punch.

The River Surveyed

Marc Alyn—Lawrence Durrell, you are so widely read now, all over the world, that one rarely meets anybody who doesn't at the very least know your name. When I was abroad recently, right in the middle of the Balkans, I went into a large international bookshop, a veritable delicatessen of the printed word, and I was struck by the amount of space given over to your books, not only in the English section, where they occupied several shelves, but also in translation in practically every other section, including very little-spoken languages. Faced by this prodigious proliferation of your thought, do you ever get the feeling that you are a sort of Tower of Babel?

Lawrence Durrell—One word comes to mind: cancer. The multiplication of healthy cells. A motor that can't stop. It's very sinister.

M.A.—A surfeit of life. Death from an excess of vitality.

L.D.—What was it Balzac said? 'Too much light. Call the doctor, quick!'

M.A.—In fact everything about you is excessive. Overabundant. Your books, the number of heroes and their complexity, the range of situations into which you throw them.

You write the same story four times over; and each

time the plot is different, extending the previous one while at the same time contradicting it. Now, in *Tunc* and *Nunquam* you have produced a double-decker novel, like a London bus built to accommodate twice the number of passengers, or in your case twice the number of characters. . . . Where does this voraciousness come from?

L.D.—I don't know. If I knew that I'd stop writing. At the beginning, you see, I was absolutely obsessed by my neurosis. The act of creation was nothing more than a therapy, a medicine for internal use, to see things more clearly, to find a way out. Miller, Seferis, me, we none of us ever dreamed that we would become famous. As far as we were concerned everything that happened, happened within a narrow, familiar framework, rather like a Greek village. As for fame, we never dared think about it; the most we could hope for was that one day our books might make us a few pennies. If some astrologer like Conrad Moricand had predicted then that Seferis's poems, Miller's *Colossus of Maroussi*, or my own stories would have had such repercussions in the future, we'd have laughed in his face. Today the real 'colossus' is overwhelmed by the fame brought him by the book: he is just a character invented by Miller. 'It's all over,' he says, 'we're clowns!' The same sort of thing has happened to me since I was 'invented' by the French, by Giroux.

M.A.—Your translator, Giroux, is first and foremost a poet.

L.D.—I consider him a highly important French poet, yes.

M.A.—In what way did he invent you?

L.D.—I was joking, but there is a good reason behind it

16

which is to show how essential the question of translation is. With a bit of luck one can always be translated accurately, but the process of transplantation is something else.

M.A.—It is strange that your translator should be the archetypal poet of the empty page—one of the 'difficulty-of-writing' school (in the sense that Cocteau speaks of the 'difficulty of being')—whereas you would seem to be a born writer, a natural sentence-maker. . . .

L.D.—That's just it. He must have sensed my impotent side! What he also sensed, and this is more serious, was the gnostic, cathar aspect that I studied on the spot (in Syria, Egypt, Palestine etc.) and which is the hidden weft of the *Quartet*. You see, Marc, when I started, I wanted to set my novel in a purely historical plane, using Alexandria as a foundation, one of the real nerve-centres of our civilization. And as I went along, through all this ordure, through this orgy, I stumbled on what is perhaps the most interesting part: the pure and dedicated quest for a new asceticism. In trying to understand that, I studied all kinds of religions—secret religions as well as openly practised ones. I couldn't help coming across the gnostics, the original Christians, the precursors, as it were, of the cathars. This is what fascinated Giroux and made it possible for him to produce such marvellous results. Because not only does he translate me absolutely accurately, he also goes further than that, he remodels me, reinvents me. And when it comes to slang or puns, he often comes up with absolute gems in French.

M.A.—There's no doubt that it needed a poet, a man of words that is, to grasp your tone, always of a poetic nature, and to make it vibrate in another language. From that point of view one can consider the *Quartet* as one huge sentence, moving in both senses, rather like the Nile sweeping along with it mud, fishes, gold, beasts, visions and legends; for though the River God is Water, he is also Time, History, Memory. . . .

L.D.—The river image is absolutely fundamental in my work: the unfurling of metaphors in the sands of everyday life.

M.A.—Already in *The Black Book* we find the river. It is as though you felt that for its layers to be properly shaken up, language needed to pass through this liquid and symbolic movement.

L.D.—Or else it's the sea. Fresh water, salt water, such a lot of water for an Irishman!

M.A.—The river—whether it be memory or space, or memory in space, or indeed memory *of* space—features in all your books, and always, to return to my earlier point, marks the moment at which the writing moves up into its highest, one might almost say its most 'literary', level.

L.D.—Perhaps I owe the idea to Joyce? In any case, what I was trying to do was quite different from the 'roman fleuve'! But of course one had to look for the river in order to get there. In short, one had to have studied Proust and Joyce and then forgotten them.

M.A.—The river as opposed to the 'roman-fleuve'?

L.D.—Precisely. Precisely. We are beset by intuitive images the whole time. You must either put them together or put them aside. The best thing, if you can do it, is to check them within the movement of the sentence itself as it takes shape; in that way you can achieve unity in duality. It's a modern discovery: consciously holding two opposing ideas in one's mind at one and the same time, and making them live side by side.

M.A.—In your novels, of course, everything is double. The story of the characters in search of an author is carried to extremes, stirred up to a frenzy. First you have the characters; then you have an author, who is also a character; and then the characters who in their way are all the authors.

L.D.—Precisely. Each one writes and is written. That's as true in books as it is in reality.

The English Death

M.A.—Lawrence Durrell, your life-story is far from straightforward. An Irishman, born in India, you went to school in England, then spent twenty years in various Mediterranean countries (Greece, Egypt, Yugoslavia) before finally ending up in France. That's a lot of moving around. To get a clearer picture of it, perhaps the best thing would be to start at the beginning with a few words about your family.

L.D.—My family had been in India for three generations. When I was born neither my father nor my mother had seen England.

M.A.—Do you still have relations in Ireland?

L.D.—I think so, but I have never made any attempt to trace them. For me, you see, Ireland is an inner space, more a state of mind than a real country.

M.A.—What sort of man was your father?

L.D.—My father was an engineer. He had been involved in the construction of the Darjeeling railway, at the foot of the Himalayas. He was an uncomplicated but determined man, as far as I remember. I must just point out that I didn't see him after I was twelve. He died while I was at school in England.

M.A.—You were born out there on 27 February 1912. Have you any lasting memories of the Indian landscape?

L.D.—An unforgettable impression, though blurred. Each morning through the dormitory windows the Himalayas would loom up out of the shadows. It was a surprise every time. How could one ever get used to a vision like that? But Mount Everest was always behind its shield of clouds. I can't have seen the Roof of the World more than twice a year.

M.A.—What characteristics have you inherited from your parents?

L.D.—From my mother I inherited the Irish side of my character: laziness and bohemianism. From my father I acquired two qualities, quite foreign to the Irish: a love of order and a sense of responsibility. I am mixture of all that. It's some inheritance!

M.A.—Your early schooling takes place in India, at the Jesuit College in Darjeeling. How did the young Durrell take to school learning?

L.D.—I was rather passive. I was inclined to believe that everything grown-ups said was true. I was a good pupil, but with no real enthusiasm or curiosity. I did, however, enjoy the physical aspect (games and sport) of school-life enormously.

M.A.—Would you say that your Indian childhood has had any lasting influence on your approach to life?

L.D.—I am, and I remain, an expatriate. That vague sense of exile has never quite left me. But at the same time it has meant that I can feel at ease anywhere, given a minimum of sunshine. The expatriate carries his country with him, inside him: everywhere belongs to him, because he belongs nowhere. Our life in India was typically colonial, i.e. very much family-orientated. The perils inherent in this sort of existence form a link between all those who have to face them. This perpetual battle with nature brings out a sense of action and duty, lacking in so-called civilized countries.

M.A.—How old were you when you left for England?

L.D.—Twelve.

M.A.—And so your English education begins. Throughout your work you express extremely critical views on England (the English Death is, after all, the underlying theme of *The Black Book*). I quote: 'That atrocious, mean little island over there, which dispossessed me of myself and tried to destroy in me all that was singular and unique. . . .'

In 1937 you write to Henry Miller, 'Fuck the English, Henry. The English are everywhere, all around me, like mutilated black beetles! I hate England.' And then in 1956 a description of the landscape: 'Everything is as serene and bland as suet!' And a little later you exclaim, 'English bastards!' I should be interested to hear chronologically how your feelings about England evolved. I imagine that this abuse conceals something altogether more complex.

L.D.—The situation has changed so much over the years, it's hard to piece it together. Or rather, no, it's quite easy. I can give a Freudian explanation for it! Here goes! It was my father who decided to send me to England. My mother was against the idea. She said I was too young, that it was cruel to send me so far away. It was the first

25

time I had witnessed a really heated argument at home; it was so calm as a rule. Seeing my mother cry was a real body-blow. But my father wouldn't give in: it was the colonial spirit, you see. He already had visions of me as a top civil servant, returning with full pomp and ceremony to help the country. In fact, these typically middle-class dreams weren't entirely negative, but they meant nothing to me. It was then that the 'transference' happened. I attack England because I identify it with my father. I immediately sensed the hypocrisy there and the puritanism, both of which have been worked over at such length that there is no point in going on about them. But I reacted with everything I had against England, primarily in order to break my father's will.

M.A.—Did it represent some sort of punishment for you?

L.D.—I must admit that I was terribly spoilt by my mother in India. Being exiled to England severed that bond. Letters went by sea then, and took six weeks to get from the metropolis to the Empire. Added to which there was the contrast between the two ways of life: Tarzan thrown head-first into the constricted world of the English!

M.A.—So the ape-man turns writer to leap, not from tree to tree like Tarzan, but from sentence to sentence, breaking out of his prison into the wide-open spaces.

L.D.—When I first started to write I was very struck by one of D. H. Lawrence's essays which showed up just how that country treated its writers. That was what made me resolve always to swim against the current.

M.A.—But do you see that as a purely English phenomenon? When you get down to it, don't you find that every creative artist is an exile in his own country? Every poet is condemned first by his time and then by the people of which he is part. Take Nerval, Baudelaire. . . .

L.D.—That's different. True masterpieces are so far ahead of their time that one can't really complain. It takes the public fifteen years to begin to recognize a work, which all that time has been concealing the magnetism of a spirit (its radar), fifteen years. . . .

M.A.—The French and the English do none the less take a very different view of their great artists.

L.D.—Look at Wilde!

M.A.—The English poet tends to flee his country, whereas his French counterpart will, more often than not, stick it out. Baudelaire made only one major trip, and that was under pressure from Aupick; Nerval did his travelling in the mind rather than across continents: everything always winds up in Paris.

L.D.—It's not surprising. You've got an absolute paradise here. I don't mean that a writer's life is 'paradisiac', far from it. But France is the *sanctuary*. You don't have the layers and layers of stupidity that we have to put up with in England—we are particularly well endowed in that area! I suppose that as far as creativity goes we are on a level with other countries. But the public!

M.A.—Not gifted, the public?

L.D.—The public has neither taste nor sensuality. In France the difference between a good Camembert, a good glass of wine and a good poet has been well established for a long time.

27

M.A.—The classicism of Camembert!

L.D.—Precisely. When one achieves fame, one becomes like a great Camembert. It's marvellous.

M.A.—While we've been talking you've been tracing a network of lines on that piece of paper. What is it supposed to be?

L.D.—The Large Intestine.

M.A.—Is there a caption underneath?

L.D.—Yes. I've written 'Durrell, a farce of nature . . .'. You see, Marc, ever since I was born, there has been one thing that has really troubled me: the Sublime. And I refuse to abandon that notion. I'm worn out now, old hat . . . [laughs]. No, what I really mean is, I'm a romantic. Nowadays it's not done to be a romantic. But I've never stopped being one, isn't it odd? In culture, in love, in everything, you must always look for the maximum you can find.

M.A.—And yet, you are a violent romantic?

L.D.—Nonsense!

M.A.—To get back to your life-story. You go on with your schooling, plus all the various intellectual and emotional adventures that you mentioned earlier. . . .

L.D.—Schools in those days were still rather Dickensian in atmosphere. The learning that was handed out to the boys mattered less than a sort of character-moulding: some of the reflexes that one picked up then—both positive and negative—stuck for a very long time. I learned one basic thing, though, which has saved my life more than once, and that was never to lose one's sang-froid. We were subjected to a total training programme based on that: the famous British phlegm is the product of a certain type of schooling.

M.A.—You started to write very early. When did you publish your first poems?

L.D.—I can't remember now. Bit by bit I forget the facts about myself. I'm packed, like a tube-train in the rush-hour. Alternatively you could say I was a galley slave. Occasionally I find myself having to look up a reference book to discover when I went to such and such a place. I couldn't give a damn personally. . . .

M.A.—One thing that seems certain is that your first steps as a poet coincide with the premature end of your education.

L.D.—At seventeen or eighteen, I was anti-everything. And yet I should have liked to have gone to Oxford, if only to give my father some pleasure. Intellectually I was brilliant, but like all Irishmen I was dreadfully lazy. And above all my subconscious was set on proving to my father (who wanted more than anything else in the world to see me go up to Oxford) that it was unfair to send me back to prison. So in spite of my capabilities I fluffed all the exams; three, four, five times. It was clear by the end that I was good for nothing. Of course I hadn't read Freud at the time, or had anything to do with psychiatrists as I do now; it was a natural complex: I deliberately failed the exams, because of a subconscious resentment, in order to prove that the initial decision was wrong.

M.A.—And did Oxford mean a great deal?

L.D.—It did to my father, certainly. What it was, was an enclave where a boy went, having got away from school, to be treated like an adult. All that was required of you was that you read a few books; it was a marvellous system: five undergraduates to one tutor, who was a specialist in literature or whatever subject you were doing. Once a week you could read an essay and discuss it with your tutor for three hours. As a principle of education it was remarkable. Of course one came across rich young men, idiots or night-clubbers who took no interest in anything; they just used to send a note saying 'I can't make it'; and so they would go for three or four years without ever seeing their tutors, and end up failing finals. But they didn't give a damn! Oxford was the gateway to the world; it was up to you whether you worked or not. But I failed to get into that magic circle—as my father called it—and all because of him. . . .

M.A.—There is an echo of this fascination with Oxford in *Mountolive*. Nessim's father is infinitely proud of having his son at Oxford. Is this a symbolic echo of the satisfaction that your own father would have felt?

L.D.—Clearly. But the period I am talking about is past now, so long ago that it might as well be the Middle Ages. To have been at Oxford or Cambridge then—to one of the major universities—gave you a cachet, something out of the ordinary, particularly as far as jobs were concerned. There was so much snobbery surrounding it, that even if you had failed every exam, you still had the social cachet. That was what my father was after. You see what sort of a man he was? The bourgeois with ambitions towards the aristocracy. It was part of something much bigger of which Oxford was the keystone. The fact remains that I missed out on three years at university, never mind which one. So there was a time-lag between me and my contemporaries. It was then that I decided to write. Before long I had joined the world of London bums.

M.A.—Writing as a substitute for the middle-class education? Bohemia instead of Oxford?

L.D.—Yes, I suppose so.

M.A.—And so we find you playing jazz in a London night club, the Blue Peter.

L.D.—Very smart.

M.A.—A way of making a living?

L.D.—Quite. I was on my uppers at the time. You know, if you're not on your uppers at eighteen, it's absurd. All we ate was chips, washed down with a couple of pints of beer, when we could borrow the dough. I was perfectly capable of sleeping in the street. A tramp's existence, I suppose you might call it.

M.A.—Had your family cut you off after the Oxford failure?

L.D.—No, no. Nothing like that. My father had died and my mother had come to live in London. . . .

M.A.—Had there been a reversal in the family fortunes?

L.D.—No. My mother was still fairly comfortably off. I knew that if things got too bad, I could always go and live with her.

M.A.—But you refused, as a matter of pride?

L.D.—I had decided that I had to stand on my own feet. That sort of decision is all the more difficult the more spoiled you have been, and I hadn't really grasped that. Only by looking back on it can I begin to see it more clearly. Just for the record, though, I always paid my debts and I never got mixed up in any scandal. More's the pity!

M.A.—Do you regret it?

L.D.—You have to do that sort of thing when you're young, you know.

M.A.—You may not have been creating scandals, but you were creating in another direction. Nowadays, wouldn't you say it's the reverse that happens?

L.D.—No, I think rather that we are moving away from individual creativity towards collective creativity.

M.A.—Do you think there's any hope of this contemporary magma of gestures and rejections shaping up into a culture?

L.D.—It's already doing so.

M.A.—People always talk about *living* culture, which seems to imply that culture can die, like any other organism?

L.D.—What does it matter? We are befuddled with words. And you French especially, you are dominated by rhetoric.

Kalymnos

Rhodes

M.A.—As far as you're concerned, a question like 'Is culture mortal?' is no more than a piece of rhetoric?

L.D.—The problem with French is that one must always be specific. What exactly do you mean by culture?

M.A.—The spiritual element that man adds to the material world. The sum total of inventions, dreams, works of art, that he leaves behind for the rest of mankind, separate from himself and yet bearing his imprint.

L.D.—Personally I see it as the fancies of the few who want to make themselves bigger; and climbing up, tearing down, imagining, acting, are all very necessary. From that point of view I think that the young today are on firm ground. There will always be an intelligentsia.

M.A.—Don't you think that the intellect is being threatened by the increasing use of drugs?

L.D.—It's a manifestation of impotence. But equally if you allow too much sexual freedom, for example, you reach a point of impotence. Give a two-year-old a bottle of gin, and naturally it will be too strong for him! It's just the same on the sexual level. I am convinced that there is a profound link between sexual and psychic energies. You haven't got on the one hand psychology and on the other metaphysics, occasionally crossing paths. . . . That of course is the reason I slept with Sartre!
(laughter)

M.A.—What about the positive values of the young today?

L.D.—The young are far more idealistic than we were. But, poor things, they need a war; what they want, if only they realized it, is for the older generation to provide them with a war. They are also more honest, when it comes to the point, but the whole situation is too complex. They have nothing, and they want an opportunity to show their strength.

M.A.—One last point on this subject—a word or two, perhaps, on the attitude of the younger generation towards writing. Culture means, above all, *memory* and, up until now, the book has in effect been man's memory. Now one gets the impression that the book is being abandoned, without as yet having been replaced (whatever people might say) by audio-visual means of communication.

L.D.—It's bound to happen.

M.A.—Do you view the rejection of reading as a good thing?

L.D.—No. Nothing is good. Everything is bad.

Corfu,
the Rectangle
and the Circle

M.A.—In 1935 you leave England and its 'ancient parapets' to go and live in the Mediterranean on Corfu. Why Corfu?

L.D.—I had decided to drop everything, and the only place where one could live on next to nothing then was Greece, especially the islands.

M.A.—Meanwhile you had married Nancy and in 1940 she presented you with a daughter, Penelope. What did you live on in Corfu?

L.D.—My mother gave me a bit. Ten pounds a month. That was for three years. On that the only place I could live was Greece. But travel or bottles of whisky were out of the question, it was impossible to do anything.

M.A.—In your early letters to Henry Miller you give a bank as your address.

L.D.—Yes, it was like Sommières where I have a P.O. box. The bank was thirty miles from the village where I lived; I went over three times a week. The Greek postal service was so unreliable, there was no point in giving a private address.

M.A.—So in short you made use of the bank's official

postal channels, just as later you carried on your correspondence via the diplomatic bag?

L.D.—Exactly. I lived like a fisherman in Corfu. It was the end of the world. One couldn't possibly find anywhere as remote in France. Once the rains started in autumn the roads were cut. There was no way of getting anywhere, either by road or by sea: the fishing boats stopped going out. So one had to make do for oneself. It was harsh, but the harshness made it enjoyable.

M.A.—You could write in peace.

L.D.—I did nothing else. I swam a great deal, I went out with the fishermen. We ate what we fished, anything that we managed to pull out of the sea. For the equivalent of ten shillings I had rented a deserted, virtually derelict house. During the winter we kept each other warm. I had married very young.

M.A.—And so you discover the Mediterranean which is to have such a hold on you. Never again do you leave its charmed circle of sun and sea. Greek blue and the ochre of Egypt will be the dominant colours in your books.

L.D.—The Mediterranean is the capital, the heart, the sex organ of Europe. Even if you ignore all the historical references, 'matrix of civilization' etc.; it is still, as it always has been, the central point, the pivot. It was quite by chance that Corfu was the first place I went to. I might easily have picked some more remote Greek island. The Ionian Islands, you know, were under British rule for nearly a century. Victorian patterns of behaviour were deeply entrenched everywhere except in metropolitan Greece, where things were still much more primitive. Compared to Athens, Corfu was like . . . Florence.

M.A.—So you settle in what can only be called the British Mediterranean?

L.D.—No. It wasn't the Englishness that mattered, but the communications, the postal service, the degree of civilization.

M.A.—When it comes down to it, you have always been concerned for your comfort. You like your wilderness in civilized surroundings. I would say this is pretty characteristic of you.

L.D.—Alexandria fulfilled that dream to perfection. It was the only place in the Mediterranean where you could still find the remains of a Venetian aristocracy. There is something Italian even about the vegetation. The Greeks used to say, 'Oh, pouah! You like these cypresses, so lukewarm. . . .'

M.A.—But Rhodes and the Dalmatian coast are also typically Italian.

L.D.—Yes. There too you come across strata of different cultures—forgotten, overlayed, covered up; people shut away in huge, deserted villas; barons, countesses, their hearts weakly beating to the rhythm of the past. Romanticism! As I've told you already, I'm an incurable romantic.

M.A.—And so, in the heart of Mediterranean civilization, an aristocracy survives, out of its time, struggling to go on and steadily declining.

L.D.—That is Alexandria in a nutshell.

M.A.—This also raises a question of political ethics. No

one reading your work could fail to discern in you a supporter of social hierarchy.

L.D.—Quite true. Taking things at the biological level, I am forced to conclude that nature is an out-and-out snob. You have only to let things follow their natural course, in your village or in your garden, and they will sort themselves out into some kind of hierarchy. There is nothing fascist about this. It is the Platonic ideal: the dog's head *knows*, but the tail is as necessary as the head. Starting from that point, you arrive at a society, more or less complex, which is able to function. Our logical systems are all based on the rectangle. And besides, the word 'system' implies a Cartesian approach, whereas societies are highly dangerous *organisms*.

M.A.—Living matter, and with a spirit as well?

L.D.—Yes, life, not systems at all. We must make use of all that we have learnt, all that we are able to learn. I say that it is essential to use the intellect to its fullest extent. If you compare all the various successive systems that have existed in the world, you will see that the deciding factors have been matters of choice, strict population control, and hierarchies.

M.A.—It seems to me that what you are talking about is not so much a monarchy or a dictatorship, as a jumble of castes, like for example those of the Ancient Egyptian priests, with their knowledge of the mysteries.

L.D.—Listen: it is quite possible that not all those priests were good at geometry, but they turned out to be as necessary to the geometrician as to the peasant. It is a voluntary uniformity in which each one does what he is best at.

M.A.—But don't you find this notion of *conserving*, rather than adding to one's heritage, somewhat disquieting, of maintaining the *status quo* without creating anything new?

L.D.—Our states, our political systems are structures that can be manipulated this way and that as much as you like. What one forgets is that one is dealing with dangerous organisms that should be approached with care and metaphysical understanding. What is needed is a sort of biological theology. . . . The American system cannot conceive of itself without its mystical bankers, any more than communism can conceive of itself without a bureaucracy. When one says this sort of thing, there's always someone who comes up with the reply, 'What you want is a dictatorship.' No. Never.

M.A.—In your *Private Correspondence* with Henry Miller, you disagree with the humanistic, egalitarian, somewhat Utopian ideals of the author of *The Air Conditioned Nightmare*. At the time you are working in a socialist country and you write back to Miller, 'Your old shoes would fetch twelve dollars here on any street.'

L.D.—I believe in Man-King-of-the-Universe. Otherwise all is lost—culture, pleasure, poetry.

M.A.—Recently, someone in the theatre, who is generally thought of as left-wing, wearily admitted in a radio programme: 'When it comes to the point, I am not certain that democracy is good for the arts.' What do you think?

L.D.—All systems are good for the arts. It is possible to work regardless of the régime.

M.A.—One mustn't confuse creating and reaching a

public. One can write poetry even in prison, but who would dare call that an ideal situation for creative work? In order to fulfil himself a poet needs both movement and stability, people and solitude, views of the universe and of 'inner space'; but what his art needs, above all, is the freedom and the leisure to tune into the inner voices. From that point of view the level of civilization in any social system can be assessed by the nature of its relationship with the artist.

L.D.—Yes, but once a thing is over and done with, you have to build a new structure to contain the seed of these ideas, a rectangular structure.

M.A.—The perfect form in your eyes is the rectangle, rather than the circle?

L.D.—The rectangle is the system; the circle is the organism. The struggle for our culture is played out between the two forms. And the tragedy is that we need them both. We are caught.

M.A.—Between the circle and the rectangle?

L.D.—Yes. One must try to fit the rectangle inside the circle, which represents health, in the Pythagorean sense. Health equals balance. One cannot simply abandon the intellect and all the riches that we have amassed throughout history. That would be absurd. On the other hand there is always the threat of an *excess* of intellectualism. We must add something better than second-rate mysticism; I don't know what. This is the kind of thing that inevitably happens: once a civilization begins to secrete too much intelligence, you find the same sort of lunatics springing up as you had in the Middle Ages. I am against that too. Man requires nourishment for both aspects of his nature.

The Black Book,
the War

M.A.—In August 1935, after reading *Tropic of Cancer*, you write your first letter to Henry Miller. It marks the beginning of an extraordinary, lifelong friendship between you. Your real literary work dates from that meeting—through letters at first—with Miller.

L.D.—I was bowled over by that book. The *Tropic of Cancer* was like a volcanic eruption; verbal larva. It was obscene but brilliant. Miller was completely unknown then, and was happy to reply to a letter.

M.A.—If you had to describe Miller in a few words, how would you do it?

L.D.—I would quote Socrates: 'I have told you that I was born many.'

M.A.—The main theme of your correspondence with Miller at this time is the book that you were writing, *The Black Book*, visionary prose, that you yourself jokingly describe as 'a book that Huxley could have written if he were a mixture of Lawrence and Shakespeare.' What would you say was the main argument of *The Black Book*?

L.D.—It puts the case for the difficulty of self-liberation. The problem was to make of oneself an open wound so as to reach a point from which to overcome the twisted

45

aspects of one's personality. I admired that in Miller; a certain contempt for literature which ends by turning it into a therapy. To free oneself of tensions. Such a project was rather a philosophical one, religious even, although I dislike the word. If the truth be told, I came very close to madness. It was absolutely vital for me to face up to these problems. Impossible then to fall back on Freud and Jung, etc., who have been such a help to me since.

M.A.—Where would you rate *The Black Book* now in your work?

L.D.—When I reread *The Black Book*, I can't see any significant changes on the poetic plane. But it is amusing to look back on that poor chap with his typewriter. That was the birth of Mr Lawrence Durrell. . . . In that book I drained the electric charge. The act of attacking oneself liberates the reader. He sees a reflection of himself. 'So,' he says to himself, 'I'm not mad after all; here's someone else who has experienced the same hidden, twisted, agonizing sensations.' But it's a path everyone has to go along. The words used by the creative person are not different from other men's.

M.A.—It is the way he shapes the words into sentences, the sentences into ideas, that is quite different. . . .

L.D.—And also the scale! We describe giants and freaks in order to illustrate instincts and inclinations that are infinitely more attenuated in real life. But the monsters exist in every one of us.

M.A.—Lawrence Durrell, or the aesthetics of enlargement?

L.D.—Excellent! You see, Marc, the thing that is

hardest to bear nowadays is that people haven't got sufficient respect for the work that we are doing. One is so bombarded by second-rate artists, journalists, officials, or by unimportant activities, that it's very difficult to concentrate on those rare beings who can give one something. . . .

M.A.—In your correspondence with Miller, we can follow the development of *The Black Book* right through to publication. What happened with this book? It almost seems as though you lost your nerve at the last minute about publishing it?

L.D.—The fact of the matter is that I was torn. The English admired it a great deal and wanted to publish it, but with a few asterisks; it was really a matter of principle. The French decided to take it as it was without any alterations or cuts. I had to choose between the two. And yet there wasn't anything particularly outrageous in it (especially when you compare it to Miller's first book!), after all T. S. Eliot, who was highly respectable, agreed to write the preface.

M.A.—But, if *The Black Book* had been published in England,* wouldn't there have been a risk of it becoming a preface by T. S. Eliot, followed by a work by Durrell?

L.D.—Eliot's courage in this affair was remarkable. He was effectively staking his literary reputation.

M.A.—You wrote at the time on this: 'First they agreed to let the word "fuck" stay in if it went thus: f—k; then f—; now the libraries might get touchy so they want —. Or something milder.'

L.D.—Precisely.

* *The Black Book* was finally published in England in 1973

47

M.A.—And yet the book as it appeared in France didn't contain anything very 'violent' in the way of language.

L.D.—It seemed so at the time.

M.A.—And did you in fact make any cuts?

L.D.—Didn't touch a thing. The text is absolutely intact.

M.A.—As soon as he had finished reading the manuscript Miller was heaping praise on you. He practically compared you to God. . . .

L.D.—Don't forget that hardly anyone had heard of Miller then. It was rather as if a Mr Smith of Leeds had said those things. Whereas Eliot's reputation was worldwide, he had been proposed for the Nobel Prize, etc. He really was risking something by defending a young man of twenty-four. He was staking his kingly reputation, his papal supremacy. Miller was a Paris bum, a beatnik. Mr Miller, who's he?

M.A.—Your attitude towards the great names of contemporary English literature has gone through some changes. But it seems to me that you have always admired Eliot, quite unreservedly.

L.D.—Eliot, you know, was an American, of British origin, who returned to live in England.

M.A.—Is that unusual?

L.D.—Henry James returned to his origins in the same way: a sort of American uprooting; he was terrifically

P.111 — A brandon.

P.117 — Unasked.

Measurement
Linear

P.135.

P.13 7. Farewell,

P.138

er. Complete :

P.144 ... Process ✗

P.147   world >

$\overline{EF}$ Is _____ centimeters
            long.

P.15 0 — Actualizes

_____ _____

AB is _____ .

p. 61 — Image Recall

p. 77 — Happiness

p. 86 — Romantic

p. 89 — Poetry   p. 98 Boredom
p. 91 — the best yet.   p. 100 Balance
                        p. 102 Feeling
                        p. 103 treasure
pc. + I.R.   p. 108 idea

Principle of relativity in dev. dif attitudes
___ under dif. conditions

Using Image Recall with a group, you
can divulge or uncover
most (of the) essential principles
that experts write about or
research shows on most any
subject (death, test, grapes, etc.)

proud the day he received a prize which was roughly equivalent to the OBE!

M.A.—And so, after several setbacks and delays, *The Black Book* is finally brought out in Paris in 1938, by Miller's publishers: this strange Englishman, who specialized in publishing in France Anglo-American books that were banned in England and America, was Kahane, alias Girodias. What was he like?

L.D.—A strange bird with an enormous beak. A typical Manchester Jew. He lived under the constant threat of deportation for publishing pornography: the French government had their eye on him. He had written four novels of his own, not in the least bit obscene, but to Anglo-Saxon ears the titles had a suggestive ring. Perhaps in memory of his friendship with James Joyce, he started to branch out into a better sort of book: Miller, Anais Nin, myself. . . . Later his son carried on with it, though not very seriously; it was thanks to that that after the Liberation the American army were able to take the *Tropics* home from Paris. And so gradually American universities got round to studying Miller's work!

M.A.—You visited Miller yourself in Paris in 1937, during the Villa Seurat periods. It was then that you, Henry and Alfred Perlès founded a review, proclaiming itself to be 'non-successful, non-political, non-cultural', which was pretty original. What memories do you have of this stay in France?

L.D.—Perlès has written all about that in his book of reminiscences *My Friend, Henry Miller*. A crazy time, but happy in spite of the difficulties. Miller toiled away like a monk, cleaning the keys and cogs of his typewriter every morning before sitting down to work: like a paid assassin checking and oiling his gun. As for Perlès, he had been manager of a billiard hall for millionaires. We used to sell subscriptions to the review in cafés and then drink what we had collected.

M.A.—This is the period when you exchange such wierd notes with Miller as: 'Dear Miller, Two questions: (1) What do you do with the garbage? (2) When you say "to be with GOD" do you identify yourself with God?'

This comes fairly close to surrealism which you say you dislike: in fact you have established a rival movement, of which you yourself are the leading spirit (and, unless I am mistaken, the only member)—'Durrealism'! What was it that you had against Breton and his friends?

L.D.—I didn't know very much about the work of the surrealists, but I felt that there was a certain *avidity* about the movement, which inevitably led it towards politics; it was that mainly that I was wary of.

M.A.—The Parisian interlude was in fact fairly short in spite of the marvellous anecdotes about it immortalized by Perles and Miller. It wasn't long before you returned to Greece and in 1939–40 got a teaching job at the British Institute in Athens and then in Kalamata. Were you a good teacher?

L.D.—I had a talent for it. I was fairly bored and often irritable, but I had a knack of sparking off six or seven minds in a class of forty pupils, I would fire arrows at them, question-marks; I taught them how to look. Those who are destined to look must work by themselves. Go and read books!

M.A.—What made you go into teaching?

L.D.—Shortly before the war, the Ministry of Information realized that there were very few Englishmen who knew Greek. I happened to arrive in Athens and a friend said, 'You're just the man they're looking for, come along to the Public Relations Office.' I spent six months there, but I didn't get on with the director. Eventually he suggested that I take a teaching job with the British Council, which is the equivalent of . . . what?

M.A.—The Alliance Française?

L.D.—That's right. I said OK. And off I went to Kalamata. Then the German tanks turned up and we had to escape to Crete in fishing boats. Once we were there the same thing happened all over again and we escaped to Egypt.

M.A.—But I am forgetting something: Miller's visit to Greece, between the time of your stay in Paris and the war.

L.D.—Yes. It is important, because he wrote the whole of the *Colossus of Maroussi* while he was there. That was at the time of the 'phoney war'; the French were lying in wait along the Maginot Line, the Germans weren't attacking; it all made for a kind of false peace, an utterly imaginary peace, since the whole world had already declared war, but no one was actually fighting it.

M.A.—That is what adds a certain strangeness to the *Colossus* of *Maroussi*; even within the context of Miller's work, which is absolutely unique, this book has a very individual ring to it.

L.D.—Quite, that comes largely from the atmosphere of the period. The actual stay was quite short: about four months. But Henry soon got to know everybody in Athens. Between times he went to Corfu where he stayed with my family before they returned to England. But the climate in which all this took place was fascinating. War or peace? Imagine, you could still telephone Germany, although the frontiers had already been closed.

M.A.—What effect did all that was happening (or not happening) have on you as a writer?

L.D.—I was fascinated by the German influence in the Balkans, and as I spoke good Greek, I managed to find out a bit about it. But there was very little one could do. As far as we could see, we were sunk. So what was there left to do? Kill oneself?

M.A.—Could one have foreseen at the time the terrible civil war that was to set Greek against Greek?

L.D.—That's the result of Sartre's influence and French culture. Cranky Communists. They were afraid. All intellectuals are cowards when it comes to action, except men like Malraux—he was not just committed intellectually, he actually fought. Of course he changed his opinions, but he did fight. If you're going to start spreading ideas in the world, you must also provide the means to act. I'm for the barricades, even for the left.

M.A.—If I understand you correctly, your view of the French intellectual is of someone spurring others on to action, while doing nothing himself?

L.D.—No, no. It's not specifically French. It's European, American, even, if you like. I reckon that if you have ideas you've got to fight for them. All too often Western intellectuals force other people either to defend themselves or to take up arms for the flimsiest reasons.

M.A.—There are times when you seem to be pursued by history, and Miller even more so. As the German advance becomes clear, we find Miller rushing round France in circles like a caged bear, without the faintest idea where to go. Even you show signs of uncertainty in your letters. 'We shall have to go there, or there, it's hard to know.' At one point your thoughts turn to Albania: 'I have filled the engine and stowed some blankets in the boat . . . also dictionary and some food, my revolver in case Albanians stray over into the bay.' There is a strong feeling of the adventure story about it all.

L.D.—You see, neither Miller nor I was politically involved, but I at least had examined the situation from that angle, and it was easier for me to foresee what the problems were likely to be. But as for Henry, he was never *there*; he was always lost in his dreams. One day he even had the idea of taking a train to Berlin, so as to go and talk to Hitler for five minutes to persuade him to abandon his military ambitions! It couldn't have been more obvious that there wasn't a hope of such a scheme coming off. But Miller was confident: 'If he could only be made to laugh, it might change everything.'

M.A.—It is true that you and Miller have quite different approaches to life. Miller doesn't take reality into account: he gives the impression of creating the world around him, according to his desires and impulses of the moment. You, on the other hand, when confronted by a serious situation, or even a dramatic one, demonstrate a very practical approach.

L.D.—I was forced to in that I had responsibilities towards a wife and a child. Henry, a 'grandiose' man in every sense of the word, had long ago decided against assuming any responsibilities; he had no one to look after apart from himself. As far as money went, he lived like a beggar; in short, he kept outside the framework of ordinary life. I, personally, couldn't do that: I was young, very much in love with my wife, and father of a lovely baby daughter. I couldn't make the sacrifices that Henry found so easy—at forty-eight. The occasion demanded that I show a modicum of intelligence in order to feed my family and get them out of what was then a very dangerous situation. Crete was under continuous Stuka fire. Aphrodite's island just missed being our tomb. It needed cunning and sang-froid to get to Egypt.

M.A.—You took the world as it was: shattered, in pieces, so confused that you could be sure of nothing, not even the worst. Miller, on the other hand, failed to grasp the full extent of the chaos into which the world had fallen.

L.D.—He was delighted to see society fucked up, but as soon as he came up against some personal problem, then he complained in the most intolerable way. He was just like a Dostoevsky character. I was a much smaller being, but then I had to act like a village notary.

M.A.—The journey from Crete to Egypt was an Odyssey in itself, wasn't it?

L.D.—The Germans had broken the lines, held by barely 15,000 men without tanks. There were less than ten planes left in Athens. They arrived with an armoured division. There was no alternative but to get out.

M.A.—The stay in Crete didn't last long.

L.D.—Six weeks, at the most. We were refugees. Everything was upside down. The port of Crete was full of sunken warships. The Nazis carried out their raid on the island with the most astonishing speed: fifteen days it took. And more intensive than on England. An attempt was made to reform, but it was hopeless. We had very few resources in Egypt that could be deployed in that sector. My friend Dudley, whom I adore, was a pilot based in Egypt with four Hurricanes. It didn't take him more than ten minutes to fly to Crete from Benghazi. So he ran a shuttle service four times a day between the island and Benghazi. Eventually the Germans shot him down. We were living under fire in barracks; fortunately I had half a bottle of whisky with me. We were in a state of total disarray, completely at a loss.

M.A.—And then you went to Egypt.

L.D.—I was with the Foreign Office at that time, which meant that I was entitled to a passage on a battleship, along with my wife and daughter. But all the ships were at the bottom of the sea, and just when there seemed no hope of getting away some drunken Australians turned up with a ship! By a stroke of luck I happened to be standing on the quay when this old tub came in. My name was on the list of people to be evacuated. 'When are you leaving?' I asked. 'This evening, if we haven't been sunk by then!' At seven o'clock we were there waiting to go on board. We were fired on during the voyage. I'll never forget one Australian who, as the shots rang out, calmly went on shaving. The following day we docked in Alexandria.

Egypt and
the First Movement
of the *Quartet*

M.A.—From 1941 to 1944 you have the job of Foreign Press Officer in Cairo; at the end of 1944 you are posted as Press Attaché to Alexandria. For the first time you enter the baroque, gaudy, sensual and putrefying universe that is to provide the backdrop to the *Alexandria Quartet*. What was Egypt like during the war years?

L.D.—An utterly artificial country, already almost an imaginary structure. In Cairo everything was open, while London and Paris were in the grip of curfews. It was marvellous. Thirty miles away there was a war going on; the soldiers used to get passes and come in for a slug of whisky.

M.A.—So, death is always at the door, just as much in the present because of the closeness of the desert and the burning tanks, as in the past (the *Quartet* is crawling with allusions to embalming, mummies, tombs . . .). In contrast to that, one gets the impression from your books that Alexandria is one vast pleasure-dome?

L.D.—It always has been like that, throughout history. But danger stirred the embers and made the passions more violent.

M.A.—To the layers of different peoples and eras— which, super-imposed one on another and yet not stifling each other, make of Alexandria a sort of living pyramid—the war brought its sands, the dust of its bones. . . . Cairo and Alexandria lay within the confines of what was one of the last remaining British strongholds in the Middle East, and the Germans were at the gates. Clearly you sublimated a great deal in the *Quartet*, but one doesn't feel very strongly the nearness of war, although it is altering and exacerbating the whole climate of the city.

L.D.—I was in such a stupefied condition all the time I was living there. And it must be nearly eight years now since I reread the *Alexandria Quartet*. I no longer remember all that well what's in it. It's hard to explain to someone of your generation how mechanical our behaviour had become by that stage, when we had quite given up. It wasn't until after the battle of El Alamein that victory began to seem a possibility. It was all over as far as we could see; it seemed as though it could take a hundred years to wipe out the Germans, they were so strong. Although they didn't admit it, that was what everyone was feeling, and it led to a sense of frustration and boredom: spleen and despair. It was neither here nor there whether one lived or died. Better dead, one thought.

M.A.—But at the same time, it put you in a situation similar to that of the condemned man, offered the opportunity to fulfil all his wishes.

L.D.—You know the story of the Englishman about to be hanged? 'One last wish?' they asked. 'I want to learn to play the violin!'

M.A.—What did your job consist of?

L.D.—It's hard to conceive. There were twelve Greek newspapers. The Greek community in Cairo was 250,000 strong; rather more in Alexandria. And on top of that there were the Syrians, the Armenians, the Turks, etc. I spent a lot of time too on the foreign press: one English newspaper, a *Paris-Soir*-type French one. Very little political stuff, no criticism of the Egyptian government. Everything was carried on in Arabic, Egyptian, Greek, Armenian. . . . That was the sector I was concerned with.

M.A.—It's while you are in Alexandria that the general outline of your great quartet of novels begins to take shape. You don't write the *Alexandria Quartet* until later, but it's clear from this letter to Henry Miller that even in 1945 you are already thinking about it: 'I have drafted about twenty pages of the new version of *The Book of the Dead*—it's about incest and Alexandria, inseparable ideas here . . .'. In fact you don't start working on it properly until you get to Rhodes in 1946, when the city—the principal character in the book—is no longer buzzing around you. That seems perfectly logical; after all it's never the actual, immediate image which is transformed into poetry but the recollected image, which needs a few months or even years in the cellars of the mind before it matures into literature. . . .

L.D.—Precisely. You need distance; you always start too soon; you think you can use a background immediately, but it never works, fortunately.

M.A.—None the less, by 1946 the style and the atmosphere are pretty clearly defined. At first the novel is to be 'a sort of spiritual butcher's shop with girls on the slabs'; but then it becomes more profound and you write: 'I am using Alexandria as a locale, and it comes

61

out bold and strong in bright colours. . . . As for style, I have developed a newish kind of prose—not surrealistic but gnomic (. . .) I am looking for a diamond-bright lucidity which will be QUOTABLE and MEMORABLE, not because of marvellous metaphors and bright lights, but because the thread of the EXPERIENCE shines through, as when you turn a tapestry round. . . '.

L.D.—I was thinking particularly of *Justine* then, but it's true that it does apply pretty well to the whole work. It took me years to evolve *Justine*, because I was having to work on so many different levels at once; history, landscape (which had to be fairly *strange* to symbolize our civilization), the weft of occultism and finally the novel about the actual process of writing. What I was trying to achieve was a canvas that was both historic and ordinary; to get that I made use of every modern technique. To my eyes, Proust had exhausted the literary potential of our society; I had to find something else, to turn, for example, to Einstein, or to go back to the origins: *The Book of the Dead*, Plato, to the occult traditions which are still alive in the East.

M.A.—You have a name for all that, the 'Heraldic Universe', an attitude of mind which consists in literarily replacing Time by Space. 'Slowly, but surely, and without conscious thought, I am destroying Time in favour of a spatial existence', you write at the time. And further on you describe 'this magic quality and this form of spatial existence that I dream of annexing to art.'

L.D.—Yes, that was what I meant when I described art as making 'sudden raids on the inarticulate.' The heraldic structure, preservation in essence, exists just as much in a sculpture as in a poem. I wanted to bring it out in the novel.

M.A.—It will be several years before the *Quartet* takes shape. Meanwhile, in 1945 you leave Alexandria and go to Rhodes, where you acquire the extraordinary, semi-royal title of Public Information Officer, Dodecanese.

L.D.—It was during the military occupation, but there wasn't a soldier at that time capable of taking on the job. As I was there and knew the language and was on good terms with some of the Greeks, they stuck me in the job. I spent two absolutely marvellous years there. I had a little jeep, and fifteen islands to visit, whenever it suited me, in a small boat—very modest but equipped with a decent motor.

M.A.—While you are in Rhodes you marry again?

L.D.—Yes, my second wife was charming. A Jewess from Alexandria. I married her because she didn't have a pass-port and at all costs didn't want to go back to Egypt. Needless to say she didn't want to get married any more than I did, but she needed papers. So I married her and, as it turned out, I didn't regret it. She had a minor job in our office, which gave her a resident's permit to stay in Rhodes, renewable every three months, but when the islands were returned to the Greeks that couldn't go on. And she hated Egypt, so . . .

M.A.—Several of your characters can't stand Egypt, including some Egyptians. Leila, for instance, dreams of one thing and one thing only: going to Europe.

L.D.—Oh! Yes.

M.A.—What was it about Egypt that made people want to get away from it?

L.D.—The deep sense of decay . . . and also the climate. Like you, I am somewhat obsessed by the effect of climate on the personality. Egypt is full of extraordinary things to look at, but the climate is exhausting; it's fantastic how 'devitalized' one becomes there. After only six months one begins to get a kind of stifled feeling. It comes from being so near the desert. You know there isn't so much as a molehill for miles around; flat as the Argentinian pampas. That's the reason I hated the Argentine so much later on; it reminded me of Egypt. I used to feel depressed after as little as ten days in Egypt. Remember the Roman poet who was exiled to the Black Sea—Juvenal? No, Ovid. . . . That was no intellectual fancy. Even small-time Egyptian clerks (it was quite a rich country) used to take themselves off to Paris once a year. Some people used to spend three or four months in Europe to let some air into the system.

M.A.—In short, after Alexandria, Rhodes for you was a sort of paradise?

L.D.—Such a relief! I have a theory about that: there are benign places and there are sterile places. Greece has always worked for me: Corfu, Rhodes, Cyprus. . . .

M.A.—And with a contrariness typical of a poet you undertake precisely to write about Alexandria. . . .

L.D.—I wrote somewhere that at one point I thought of setting the novel in Athens. But with the play of the four different times and the four volumes, I ran the risk of boring the reader by using the same background for every scene. It made it almost impossible to tell the same story several times over. Or else I should have fallen into a Musil-type 'roman-fleuve', dull as ditchwater: seven volumes of nothing, flowing on and on. . . .

64

Corfu

Rhodes (water-colour)

Sommières

Harbour scene

M.A.—Quite. It seems to me that one of the fundamental ingredients, apart from the narrative, in the *Quartet* is precisely that fascination with writing which affects both characters and writer at all levels. The *Quartet* is also, in the Goethian sense, an 'apprentice' novel, the account of a literary vocation. I detect in it a mixture of instinctive confidence as to the direction in which it is going and a certain wavering between pure literature (poetry) and best-seller writing. If I'm not mistaken it was some popular novels, written under a pseudonym, that first got you accepted by Fabers.

L.D.—That's right. I had written my first novel when I was eighteen. It was vital for me to prove to my family that I was a writer, and for non-creative people the real test is whether or not you make any cash from it—you must know that as well as I do! Everyone said, 'All you do is play the piano in night clubs. . . .' At that time my poems weren't worth reading, they were very naïve. After all, I *was* naïve, at eighteen, what can you expect? But it's easier to write a commonplace novel than it is to write good poetry. Once I realized that, I said to myself: Right, if I can find someone to publish a novel by me, that'll prove to them that I have got a vocation. And it worked. When they saw the cheque (a very small one: forty pounds), I could see that I had succeeded, more especially as the book actually appeared. Like everyone else I went through a rather beatnik period, but I had my feet a little too firmly on the ground even then.

M.A.—Yes, there is a strange similarity here between the young beatnik, Lawrence Durrell, and François Mauriac, the young bourgeois. Mauriac in fact claimed that both his literary beginnings and his subsequent delight at being awarded the Nobel Prize stemmed from the same desire to amaze (or convince) his family in Bordeaux.

L.D.—Absolutely. But then I can see this same typically adolescent confusion in Boris Vian, or Malcolm Lowry, who loved jazz but didn't play as well as me! He wasted his time writing songs, but without much to show for it. Like Boris Vian he was a bit *jazzed up*.

M.A.—In spite of everything this taste, dare I say it, for the 'popular novel', continued for a while.

L.D.—The thing was, I wanted to produce something that would be readable on a superficial level, while at the same time giving the reader—to the extent that he was touched by the more enigmatic aspects—the opportunity to attempt the second layer, and so on. . . . Just like a house-painter; he puts on three, four coats. And then it starts to rain, and you see the second coat coming through. A sort of palimpsest.

M.A.—That's how I see it.

L.D.—But the bore was that I succeeded in attracting a great many readers who understood absolutely nothing, apart from one or two of the more brilliant scenes: they were attracted without knowing why.

M.A.—At the time of *The Black Book*, Miller reprimands you pretty severely for trying to play two tunes in different keys. There's no doubt that he was right to urge you to choose invention and poetry. But perhaps the *Quartet* would never have had such a vast readership were it not for those early experiments in 'light' literature, which you later suppressed? I would say that the fact that at a certain period in your youth you were capable of writing that type of book—not as easy as people make out, particularly for a poet—explains something about the more 'popular' aspect of your writing.

66

L.D.—It's more a question of a deep psychological weakness. I'm too excitable, and that means that I'm always going from one form to another. For instance, if I find that I can't write, I that have come up against a brick wall in the work that I am doing, I immediately turn to painting, or a bit of musichall. Everything I do is an orgy. And this weakness was even more pronounced when I was young, which explains the numerous attempts I have made to plumb deeper into various genres: the novel, music, poetry. Playing jazz on the piano is both a relaxation and a therapy. As soon as I had pin-pointed this central weakness in my character, I realized that if I didn't move constantly from one art form to another, I should never be able to relax.

M.A.—Yes. Everything about you is a series of scales.

L.D.—But great men show a patience that I have never had. It is a serious fault in my makeup. Poems can't be forced—they are like stalactites, you have to wait for them, be worthy of them. Sometimes you might have to wait twenty years for a poem. I was too impatient. I wanted to swallow everything—and naturally. . . . Well, there you have it!

Winged Heels

M.A.—What stage have we reached now in your literary career? In 1943 and 1946 you successfully published two volumes of poetry in London. On the prose side, you continue to work on *Justine*, but your job doesn't leave you enough time to make any real progress in this long and exacting work; and so, on the side, you write a strange story, *Dark Labyrinth*. A modern version of the myth of the labyrinth, isn't that right?

L.D.—Yes. It's a short novel. But what is in it? It's five years since I last looked at it. Ah yes, allegory! I hate allegory. Some tourists who lose their way in the labyrinth in Crete, and the Minotaur has just returned. . . . But then for ten months I also worked on *Sappho*, a play, which has been produced in Germany. That *was* important.

M.A.—A poetic play, is that right?

L.D.—I can never understand this distinction between poetry and prose.

M.A.—Of course. You don't find two types of water flowing from one spring. But then maybe the springs are so rare that one should specify what it is that they cure?

L.D.—Let's have a drink!

M.A.—In 1947 you spend some time in the Argentine, a noteworthy episode in your life because it's the only time you leave the Mediterranean. What on earth took you to the Argentine?

L.D.—I'll tell you. I had just failed to get the job I wanted in Athens. There was nothing else around and I was very short of money, so I asked for anything that was going. They said, 'Would you take the Argentine meanwhile?' I had no option. 'Why not?' I said. 'It'll make a change.'

M.A.—Still with the British Council?

L.D.—Yes. I flew from village to village, talking about literature. I was director of the Institute in Cordoba, but the job consisted mostly of giving stupid lectures. . . .

M.A.—I see, lecturing on Joyce in the pampas!

L.D.—Exactly. I found the climate exhausting and the landscape boring. It was Egypt all over again, you know. No mountains, nothing, absolutely nothing, and all that basking in warm air. . . . My original decision proved to have been utterly mistaken, even though I was to meet some of my best friends there. And no political work, just cultural stuff until I was sick of it! I stayed a year and a half. When I got back to London, I said to the Foreign Office, 'I'm free. Anything for me?' And they said, 'Haven't you seen the newspapers? Tito has broken with Stalin. What do you feel about Belgrade?' I said, 'I'll take it. Give me Belgrade.' And I left that very evening.

M.A.—Your letters from Belgrade aren't very cheerful.

L.D—.It was a dismal period and a dangerous one. My

predecessor, who had resigned, said, 'It's marvellous, you can never get to see anyone!' I liked the people and the countryside in Yugoslavia, but not the system.

M.A.—And yet communism in Yugoslavia is quite different from communism in the other satellite countries.

L.D.—At that time only the aims were different; they had different ideas and aspirations, but the reality was just as sinister as anywhere else. The Stalinist grip didn't loosen from one day to the next, nor did the wretchedness of the standard of living improve. And besides, I loathe communism. The theory is non-existent and the practice horrendous. It's ill-conceived, misshapen. Any fool could tell you why it is that whenever anyone tries to institute it—and one can't deny that it is founded on splendid egalitarian ideals—it takes a police force to maintain it: people immediately sense something wrong, something dishonest behind it. People stay where they are purely because of the police and the force of arms. If it really were the Golden Age you would find freedom and kindness and a society with virtually no police force. It was a problem I had to face while I was there. I inclined vaguely towards socialism, in the sense of egalitarianism; I was all for reforms which gave everyone enough to eat and a bit more happiness. But there I saw thoroughly honest people being forced to submit to a sort of inquisition. Basically the communists themselves are the most disappointed people I have ever met.

M.A.—Your experience of Yugoslavia was at a particularly distressing period of its history. It took more than the break with Russia to root out Stalinism, foreign though it was to the spirit of Yugoslavia. The wheels of the machine went on turning for some time.

L.D.—You must forgive my egotism: I am speaking

73

purely for myself. I had never really studied Marxism until then. But my professional integrity was such that I felt duty-bound to take an interest in the affairs of the country, wherever I was posted, whether it was a communist state or the Vatican. Had it been the Vatican, for instance, I should have gone to a Dominican for instruction, read Thomas Aquinas, studied theology and the politics of the Church. And so I turned myself into a Marxist to try to see what could be understood of that precise moment in history. And, frankly, what I saw there was the betrayal of Europe's cultural heritage.

M.A.—What about the Yugoslavs themselves?

L.D.—I have nothing against them at all. They are a bit hysterical but I like that! To tell you the truth, I had a lot of admiration for them, and I still have some very good friends there. No, it was the system that got my back up. In order to get people to accept things that didn't work, they pretended to have created paradise on earth.

M.A.—So as soon as you get a chance to leave, you jump at it.

L.D.—That is all tied up with my official life. After four and a half years in Yugoslavia and all the work I had put into studying the situation, I had become something of an expert on communist affairs. Of course I couldn't give a damn about that sort of thing. Unfortunately, as far as the Foreign Office is concerned, once you have been somewhere for five years, they think that you must be frightfully clued up about the area and you always run the risk of being posted back there. They suggested Sofia, Moscow and various other capitals, all communist. But I'd had enough. It was impossible to get a job in Greece,

74

so I decided to drop everything and go and live in Cyprus.

M.A.—Why Cyprus?

L.D.—Quite simple. There were strict currency restrictions in force in England at that time. It was impossible to take money out. You've had the same kind of thing in France: 'You can take 500 francs for your yearly holiday, but try not to spend it all.' I didn't have much in England, but I had enough to live on in Greece; only the currency regulations made it impossible. But there was one Greek island, inhabited by the English, which was part of the sterling area, and that was Cyprus. From there it was easy, by letter or telegram, to get any money that I earned in London transferred.

M.A.—So from 1953 to 1956 we find you back in your beloved Mediterranean, in Cyprus, where you buy a house in a mountain village. In a very beautiful book—a mixture of reportage and poetry—*Bitter Lemons*, you describe the enchantment of this island, set against the stormy background of political upheavals. Your stay there falls into three periods: you start off by writing, then you teach, and finally you get an official job in Government House as director of Public Relations.

L.D.—That's right. I had nearly finished *Justine*. Then the crisis flared up and panic broke out.

M.A.—The creative side of your life seems to be bedevilled by problems. I remember a letter dated 1953 in which you wrote: 'I feel like one of those machines for distilled water—it is coming drop by drop. . . . This is really writing one's way upstream with a vengeance.'

75

L.D.—My job was exhausting me. The Greeks had found me a teaching post in Nicosia. I wasn't all that hard up, but just in case, I thought it was wiser to get a job until I had completed final arrangements for the house I had just bought. My books were published in very small editions: apart from the advances they never brought in any money. So I took the job. But it meant getting up at half-past four in the morning and driving to Nicosia, fifteen to twenty miles away, and then teaching from eight o'clock until four-thirty.

M.A.—And then quite soon, on top of everything else, comes the anti-British uprising.

L.D.—Enosis. One was virtually in the middle of a war. Life was becoming intolerable. I found myself torn between my Greek friends and my compatriots.

M.A.—It was then that you were offered another official job in the Government Press Office. And so you get a two-sided view of what is happening: from diplomatic circles and from among the people, the peasants?

L.D.—Yes. I enjoyed the confidence of Makarios, but there was very little one could do, on account of the sheer rottenness of the situation. The English lack of flexibility in matters of diplomacy was revealed in all its glory. When the crisis came, all they did was to replace one constitution with another. I could sympathize with the Greek point of view. But the tragedy was that most of the English didn't understand the language: they needed interpreters to translate the Cypriot slogans for them. It was not surprising that things turned out the way they did.

M.A.—The situation must have had its dangers for you too, in spite of your friends?

L.D.—There came a point when the people in the village made it clear that it would be better for me if I left. Otherwise they might have been forced, in the nicest possible way, to cut my throat. . . .

M.A.—Cyprus seems to have been a turning-point, a crossroads in your life. It was there that you wrote *Justine* and that one of the characters from the novel actually appeared in your life: Claude, a Frenchwoman from Alexandria whom you marry in 1961. Claude, too, was a writer, an important factor, which must have contributed to your decision to give up your job and devote yourself, at last, completely to writing.

L.D.—In fact I was the one who decided to come and live in France. For the first time I felt that I needed to be free. I had to make a break, had to choose: I chose to live in the south of France and try my luck as a writer.

M.A.—And so you loop the loop and we find you once more in France, in Sommières in the Languedoc. You are poor, inspired, free and in love. Are you happy?

L.D.—Infinitely. Sideways, lengthways, in every way.

M.A.—Which brings me naturally to the question, what does happiness consist of for you?

L.D.—Happiness is the complete acceptance of one's responsibilities.

Life in Sommières

M.A.—What makes you decide in 1957 to come and live in Sommières, here in the Gard, in preference to any other town in the south of France?

L.D.—I was twenty when I discovered France, and a little older when I first came to the Languedoc. I remember noting at the time that the Gard was a severe place.

M.A.—Yes, there is a harshness here which seems to stem from the landscape and communicate itself to the soul.

L.D.—When I left Cyprus, I came to Montpellier looking for a village in which to settle; that took me to Aujargues and then to Sommières. . . .

M.A.—And so this 'medieval town asleep on its feet' becomes your base, the fixed point, home.

L.D.—Even as a young man I saw that this area had the perfect atmosphere for a writer. At that time, what I dreamt of was living in Greece and spending the winter here. I have reversed the formula now: what I really enjoy is living in France and spending occasional holidays in Greece.

M.A.—It isn't long before close ties develop between you, the great traveller, and this sleepy, straggling village where you rent a house overlooking the Vidourle, to put the finishing touches to the book that has been gestating since 1945 (the *Quartet*). In one of your first letters from France to Henry Miller, you describe Sommières enthusiastically and with warmth: 'It's lovely,' you write, 'on this gracious rive, something like Stratford plus Canterbury . . .'. What did you mean by this comparison with the English countryside?

L.D.—Simply that family atmosphere that ancient little villages have when they are in harmony with the surrounding countryside. The way everything radiates from a market-place. . . . I should imagine that, in the same way, a French poet visiting England would find certain spots which reminded him of familiar places in the French countryside.

M.A.—You arrive here not as a rich tourist come to acquire a lazy Mediterranean tan, but rather as an adventurer playing out his destiny. At the age of forty-five you decide, very courageously, to give up the work that had until then provided your means of support. Did you decide on impulse or had you been considering it for some time?

L.D.—On impulse. Like someone joining the Foreign Legion. I had been writing for twenty years and had never made a penny out of it. So that my idea of living off my writing was quite mad. But I worked out that if I wrote two novels a year, with a bit of luck it might work.

M.A.—Your decision was all the more risky in that you had neither capital nor any regular source of income.

You were burning your boats: either you would storm your way to success with your novels, or else you would, socially speaking, go to the wall. Did you think that you would be able to go back to the kind of life you were leading before, if things didn't work out?

L.D.—No. But every now and again one must put oneself in an extreme situation. You get a marvellous trampoline effect from saying to yourself: It's this or death! The end product is not in itself important: simply a purge. What matters is the actual effort. Major decisions spring-clean the spirit.

M.A.—Would you like to say something about the kind of life that you lead during this period of intensive work (three novels in two years as well as articles, letters, contributions to reviews) which to the outsider appears quite fantastic?

L.D.—Luckily by then I had acquired a fair amount of experience. I was born with a typewriter in my mouth!

M.A.—That's an interesting image. . . . Your kind of writing has very close links with the spoken word.

L.D.—This experience of writing was of immediate use. Apart from that I led a monastic life—a monk with a wife though; so Claude wrote at one end of the room and I worked at the other. This extended period of solitary work didn't get me down: I was beginning to tire of social life when I made the decision. In short I turned myself into a Balzac!

M.A.—This question of your timetable is not without importance, because your public image is of the archetypal writer altering his life by the power of his imagination. Besides, you are conscious of that yourself: in the music of the *Quartet* there is always a typewriter clattering somewhere.

L.D.—I used to get up at five in the morning and start work straight away. At ten I would drop everything. You must never let even a single day go by without writing a few lines, a paragraph.

M.A.—In literary terms you are a marvellous landscape painter. One could go on for ever quoting memorable sentences and pages in your description of places. Is there a link, conscious or unconscious, between the Egyptian landscapes that you describe in the *Quartet* and the *garrigue* that you look out on while you are writing? Or did you write with the curtains drawn?

L.D.—In the *Quartet*, I drew on all my poetic resources, including word-painting. It's very difficult to construct four novels around one subject. That's why you often find three or four metaphors in one sentence. I was virtually imprisoned in the house while I was writing; added to which, I had my desk facing a wall. I also work by electric light here. When you are as lazy as I am, you must avoid any outside visual distraction. Who knows? You might catch sight of a bird or a dog, and then everything would go by the board. . . .

M.A.—Landscape apart, there are people, you write somewhere, who are 'modified' by the place in which they live to the point that they are an expression of their landscape. What were your early contacts with the people of Sommières like?

L.D.—Sommières people? They are welcoming in a straightforward sort of way, neither unforthcoming nor curious. No preconceived ideas. I like them a great deal, and I think it's mutual. To begin with Claude and I appeared as the eternal students. They took us as we were, without asking any questions. . . . Once I forgot to renew my resident's permit. The local chief of police apologized for sending for me, explaining tactfully, 'If I had sent a man over to see you, it would have made a bad impression in the town.'

M.A.—From order to anarchy now, if you don't mind. You recently completed a television film about a very delightful tramp from the region of Sommières. What was it that attracted you to Blanco (I use the past tense as he has since died in a road accident)—was it a certain image of incorruptible freedom?

L.D.—Poor Blanco! He was a character, a 'natural' as they say in films. He was the perfect Knight of the Road, one of the wanderers, the rejecters. They have their own fifteen-character alphabet. They walk.

M.A.—How do you reconcile your taste for social order, which is, as we have seen, a feature of your character, with this love for the tramp?

L.D.—The problem is: How to combine the maximum possible freedom with necessities. In a well-conceived, harmonious society, there is also room, on his own level, for the tramp, who after all abides by laws, the laws of the 'corporation'. And as for the tramps' code of honour —it's really complex! The lure of the road stems from a very old and deep-rooted feeling in man: look at the pilgrimages of the past. And yet that is one of the surprising things about them: they don't pass on religious secrets to each other. They are linked through a sort of brotherhood, but they have no songs, no oral or written

85

tradition. They are absolutely anti-creative; often sensitive to natural beauty, but with neither the memory nor the language to express it. On the other hand, they do have a highly intricate sign language for communicating practical, useful information to other initiates. Blanco showed me some of them: he would draw a line on the ground, and any passing tramps would know from that, that not far away there was a hiding-place or a cache of things to be picked up. It gave rise to this sort of dialogue between us:

'Is it like birds migrating?'

'But, monsieur, they have no choice!'

'Do you have any plans for the future?'

'Oh, no! [very shocked]. I throw my cap in the air and I go in the direction it flies in.'

Blanco was the dawn. There was another who was called Dusk.

M.A.—Always the romantic, Lawrence Durrell?

L.D.—All poets and most writers, including those who seem to be 'classical', are romantics. All creative people struggle to get back to their childhood: they hope that by following that path they will one day become adults.

M.A.—How do you yourself define romanticism?

L.D.—The romantic is forever in conflict with himself.

Poetry: A Tragic Game

M.A.—It's difficult to take in at a glance the general shape of your work (and even more so to describe it): you have written a great many books, in widely differing genres; poetry and novels; essays and humorous stories; travel articles and plays; and that's not counting the hybrid texts which can't be said to belong to any one particular form, but to all at once. Just supposing (a wild hypothesis) that you had to make a choice between these various genres, which would you select as closest to your heart?

L.D.—My poetry, naturally. The poetic form expresses what is most intimate, most profound in man as he relates to the world. It's also the most terrifying form; you have to compress into, say, three lines the most unbelievably complex experience. Poetry is all a question of density.

M.A.—Do you feel that you have gone as far as you would have wished in poetry?

L.D.—I think I've missed my shot. I should have killed myself at the age of twenty-five. . . .

M.A.—Critics have compared your style of poetic writing both to English metaphysical poetry and to contemporary Greek elegiac poetry; in short, a combination of John Donne and Seferis. What's your view on that?

L.D.—I have been profoundly influenced both by the best English poets and by the metaphysical side of the Greeks. Basically Valéry is very close to Seferis. It's the gnomic quality, the density. I feel, like them, that what matters is to say something that has meaning.

M.A.—It is true, though, that your poems are quite unlike anything else that has been written in England since 1930. Your work has a transparence, a light that one doesn't begin to find in other writers of your generation. How do you explain this difference?

L.D.—It's a question of landscape. I firmly believe in the theory that landscape shapes people and behaviour-patterns. That's why there's no Châteauneuf-du-Pape in Scotland.

M.A.—Nor whisky in Avignon!

L.D.—I have tried to see people through landscapes. A barren land won't produce fruit, so I personally didn't stay there, but travelled and found for myself. Here one must know how to be an egoist.

M.A.—Which poets of the past do you most admire?

L.D.—Shakespeare and Donne. That's counting English and French poets. And then Ovid. That's a deep-rooted complex. As a child I knew Ovid off by heart.

M.A.—And among contemporary poets?

L.D.—I've never thought about it. . . . Nowadays words are being carved up by computers. You can find something like two thousand possibilities in a three-syllable word. Take a word like 'love', for instance: you can make thousands of epigrams from it—or epitaphs for that matter. . . . I am for concrete poets. Even if it isn't poetry. I'm for them, like I'm for the Marquis de Sade. Always on the side of those who go to extremes.

M.A.—Action for action's sake?

L.D.—Take 'Lettrism'. Frankly, it isn't creative. No real meat in it, nothing to get your teeth into. But it has to be done. It is vital to have plenty of people working on the vines. One day a chap turns up and takes the lot to make his wine. One is always useful, whether one is working with the soil or with the language. Even if the end result is pathetic, one is useful.

M.A.—Yes, it's the manure that makes the tree. . . . But don't you think that exploding words into letters sometimes just gives the old dictionary a new lease of life?

L.D.—We've got far too many dictionaries, that's quite true. Think back to the time of Shakespeare, before the language had set, when it was still phonetic. Things were spelled out. The best is what hasn't yet achieved its final form. The Greeks today can still enjoy that. Their language is only a hundred years old. They reinvent their country through words. One word of Aristotle plus a bit of nonsense and you discover a new marvel. The fact is that we are over-sophisticated now. A culture has a first pressing, just like olive oil. . . .

M.A.—And subsequent ones?

L.D.—Yes. And only extreme *dryness* can prevent the over-refinement of language.

M.A.—Can you give an example?

L.D.—Beckett.

M.A.—Your own poems stand at the opposite extreme. You are elegiac. Which poem or line of a poem are you most proud of?

L.D.—One is always one's own worst critic. But I do have a certain sense of having succeeded in two poems about the *effect* of the Mediterranean landscape.

M.A.—Is it because of the theme, always identifiable? I sometimes think that in your work perfection borders on the anthology piece.

L.D.—Do you think so? I loathe anthologies. They are generally compiled by dons. For me, as I have said, poetry is a way of breathing. I never reread. New editions give me a feeling of distress.

M.A.—The solar radiation of your poems comes over remarkably well in Alain Bosquet's French translation.

L.D.—I have always been very lucky with my French translators, they bring a new dimension to my work. But then my French is so bad.

M.A.—I don't believe a word of it. Besides, didn't you once tell me that you sometimes dreamed in French?

L.D.—I wrote a whole collection of poems in French. And very bad it was too. It's called *Poèmes en petit-nègre*!* I've also written poems in Greek. When you don't know a language in depth, it's easier to play around with it.

* 'Pidgin Poems'

And as playing for me is synonymous with pleasure, it's a vital exercise. I know perfectly well that I'll never manage to create what I really want; I know I'll never be Valéry, or even some less good French poet. But I get a great deal of pleasure from playing in a language which is so much stricter that our beef stew of a language! English is like a boxer's punching-ball: you can hit it which ever way you like.

M.A.—When you talk of play and pleasure, I get the impression that instinctively your feelers are turning towards poetry rather than towards the novel. Is poetry a game for you?

L.D.—A tragic game, in a sense. I would so much like to be a poet . . . and I'm not sure that I'm up to it. Perhaps two or three of my poems will be bull's-eyes, but as far as consistence goes, I've failed, missed the boat. One can be a very good poet without necessarily being a great poet.

M.A.—There are those who would say that it is for others to judge whether a poet is great or not.

L.D.—Not at all, and you know that better than anyone. The basic principle is quite different: the principle of condensation. To achieve great poetry, you must give up everything. Personally, I have been over-greedy about life.

The Novel Versus Suicide

Sommières, Villa Louis

Turkish Women, Egypt

M.A.—What are you working on at the moment?

L.D.—I am making notes. Endless notes. Either a lot will come out of them, or nothing at all.

M.A.—At what point do you know that you have really begun a novel?

L.D.—It depends. There have been times when I have torn up two hundred pages simply to spare myself the trouble of going on with them and putting them into shape. Then I would dream about the burnt pages until they began to shape up inside me again, sometimes in completely the opposite order to the original. At that point, I would transplant them into my atmosphere.

M.A.—And right now is there a novel in the pipeline?

L.D.—Ah! No. I'm too superstitious. Once you say that a thing is there, then it disappears. . . . What I can say for certain though is that either I start a novel or I commit suicide.

M.A.—Not before the end of these interviews!

L.D.—No, don't worry. I always keep appointments. Duty holds me to life as much as pleasure does.

M.A.—You often talk of suicide, rather as though you were talking about some particularly delicious delicacy. It's not a new subject for you; in your very first book, you write, 'Youth is the age of despair. . . .'

L.D.—Look here, that hasn't changed. I'm still desperate. Action is the only way out, but it's also the most difficult. Basically most people are in despair. I can only say again, either I kill myself or I create something.

M.A.—But have you ever *really* been tempted by the idea of suicide?

L.D.—The whole time. Even now.

M.A.—Fortunately you've never got further than thinking about it.

L.D.—I suppose I'm too much of a coward. Suicide seems to me to be the only solution. In adolescence one is for ever getting lost. And the more the natural forces intensify in us, the more complexes we experience in that respect. I'm so exhausted today after erecting my monument of words that I'm in the most marvellous state for suicide. It could happen from sheer tiredness. At eighteen one doesn't kill oneself out of boredom, because boredom isn't a real factor. Now I'm conscious of spleen—it's fabulous, stunning. One could quite simply stop breathing.

M.A.—Is boredom a good conductor of self-destructive tendencies?

L.D.—But of course. It's the only one.

M.A.—And this novel which you aren't writing but which

you're spending all your time on, where is it set? Will the action (if there is any action) take place in your beloved Mediterranean?

L.D.—All over the place. No, really, I don't know. I daren't know. There are too many possibilities. It's different every time. I adore the game, but I don't know yet. This winter I'll know for sure. It takes me a hundred and fifty pages before I can decide whether a novel is coming to life, or whether there is still time to abort it. It's a case of the foetal heart. I'll go back to the beginning, but not until I have heard the heart-beat. Every day I read it through; the lorry-driving aspect of the work is essential in order to carry on. A novel, you know, Marc, is like a heavy lorry, full of people, places, cries. If the load isn't properly stowed and balanced, the whole lot tips off at the first bend. A poem, in comparison, has the lightness of an arrow.

M.A.—Exactly. The poem aims right at the heart of the absolute, the bull's-eye of some ideal target, while the novel trundles towards the crowd, towards the public. . . .

L.D.—That's it. Yes.

M.A.—Do you ever write poetry at the same time as you are writing a novel?

L.D.—Everything. All at the same time. I get so nervous whenever I reach a point where I really ought to concentrate, that I throw myself into diplomatic nonsense. I've got five or six notebooks filled with such nonsense. Circumstances dictate these changes of rhythm or genre: if the *New York Times*, for instance, has commissioned an article on the Middle East, or if I'm stuck halfway through a chapter. Then I pick up something else and start writing.

M.A.—In short, your balance lies in imbalance?

L.D.—I love to feel myself in a state of nervous tension. I sail against the wind, against windbags. I am a writer who hovers over things.

M.A.—And yet writing remains the central point in your life.

L.D.—I find writing no more amusing than making love or eating; it's not important.

M.A.—What is important?

L.D.—Me. I am a narcissist. In a state of permanent disarray, because I'm a poet. There's nothing I can do about it.

M.A.—And how about painting, is that another of your ways of exorcizing the disarray?

L.D.—Painting isn't me, it's Oscar. Oscar Epfs, my pseudonym. It is 'I', of course, as long as you remember Rimbaud's insight, 'I is someone else'. I thought that Epfs was so marvellous, he deserved an Oscar. Blown up, like all great discoveries, in Paris. Do you know that Picasso went down with flu when he heard about Epfs. Epfsistentialism, that's my philosophy.

M.A.—One of the peculiarities of Oscar's paintings (I can see one there over your desk of a string of popes) is the way they *breathe* when you turn on the heating.

L.D.—To breathe is to enjoy. Of course my painting is inflatable, washable, pulsating like life itself. Look at those popes: they've got the most enormous paunches.

I'm on a strict anti-paunch diet, because of that famous complex. I paint when I want to 'rummage' inside myself.

M.A.—And when did this titillation with paint start?

L.D.—I've always done water-colours. When I was about twenty I lived on a Greek island with a young painter. It was then that I started to look at things through water-colour. When I went to Paris, Miller encouraged me. We didn't take it very seriously: it was never going to provide us with food or drink; it was just for fun. Miller taught me how to paint masterpieces. His technique went like this: you paint a horse or a woman or any old crap; then you make for the bathroom and run it under the tap; and you've got a masterpiece! The essential point is washing the picture.

M.A.—Miller and you—sorry, Miller and Epfs—certainly introduce a new dimension into art: bringing back the wash, literally.

L.D.—Michaux is as good a painter as he is a poet. So is Miller, only he's very capricious: he was the first to recognize his own success. He always behaved like a best-seller right from the start, when he couldn't even find himself a publisher. In his mind he's already won the Nobel Prize twenty times over. It's not pride, he just doesn't give a damn for the outside world. And without any affectation either—in all innocence, he's still very much a child. He's waited twenty years for others to follow his lead.

M.A.—And others, as was only right, have followed.

L.D.—Yes. I personally immediately saw a genius in

Henry. It's pretty rare, but this man *lived* his ideas, whereas I was surrounded by people who had ideas but didn't express them in their actions. In different ways T. S. Eliot and Valéry lived their thoughts too.

M.A.—I'm glad you say that. Too many people nowadays seem to imagine that unless a poet leads a scandalous public life, he's not the real thing.

L.D.—It all depends on the way you write. Frenzied, delirious writing can demand irrational action; structured, carefully ordered writing, on the other hand, needs a calmer existence. Outwardly, at any rate. In fact, when you go deeper, the merits and the dangers are the same. I have known two great poets: Yeats and Eliot. Yeats I saw, but without ever really getting close to him. But Eliot was my editor. Henry Miller inspired me with his feeling for life, Eliot with his feeling for thought. Valéry had a feeling for poetic form, for shape. I'm talking about the men, not about their reputations. Henry was unknown then, whereas Yeats, Eliot and Valéry were regarded as the popes of literature.

M.A.—You admire such different people, how do you reconcile them all?

L.D.—I'm a literary adventurer. Personally I don't give a damn. Cendrars would affect me just the same if I hadn't read a single line he'd written. But then you see I'm Irish, which means not very normal.

M.A.—There's the man of course. But man is by nature a maker of masks. Who hides and who is hidden?

L.D.—Valéry's public image is a very dry one, but deep down there's a hidden tenderness. The same with Eliot.

Imagine a meeting between Rilke and Valéry. Men like these represent the real wealth of a period. There will perhaps be two or three in a generation who give a psychic value to the rest.

M.A.—Treasure is by definition buried, there but invisible. Not shameful, simply out of sight. Happily, a few know of its existence. Are you never embarrassed, not to say disturbed, by your popular success?

L.D.—A total stranger once came up to me in a Paris street and kissed my hand. That means a great deal. There's always someone to kindle the fire. Maybe it's just another form of narcissism.

M.A.—Your image needs a reflection, a mirror.

L.D.—I was in Hamburg once, at the invitation of some very distinguished Prussians. Precisely the sort of meeting that one ought to avoid. There was an old countess there who had once shared a flat with Rainer Maria Rilke. She told me this story: Rilke had gone to Venice to buy a mirror; when he returned he was broke, naturally, but happy. Not long afterwards the mirror disappeared, evidently filched by one of the chambermaids, a girl of exceptional beauty. Everyone expected Rilke to be inconsolable. Not at all. 'You must go to the police, bring her to justice,' they all said. But Rilke replied dreamily and with a note of admiration in his voice, 'Certainly not. Her beauty recognized something which was destined for it.'

Talking About Writers

M.A.—I've noticed that although you often talk about literature in general, you hardly ever mention particular writers by name, apart from a few favourites.

L.D.—I detest littérateurs; they are far too serious. Personally, I am a child, a footballer!

M.A.—Are you for innocence and youth then?

L.D.—No! I have a horror of youth and *naïveté*. I just hope that the young will manage to order (disorder) things in their own way, and by that I mean using a good deal of brutality, absurdity and stupidity.

M.A.—People have surprisingly strong views about hippies: either passionately for, or passionately against, nothing in between. . . .

L.D.—I have complete confidence in them, they are far more deeply idealistic that previous generations. At their age, we were *terribly* manipulated by idiots; they are breaking loose from that grip, which is good. In any case I don't give a damn. I can't stand competition.

M.A.—Is there an element of jealousy perhaps?

L.D.—It's hard growing old, when you have set as much

store by the physical side of life as I have. Oh! It's not serious yet: one is still handsome, kind, women adore one, but when it comes to chopping wood. . . .

M.A.—Is that why you do yoga?

L.D.—The great thing about yoga is that by lightening the body it liberates the mind. It helps me clear my thoughts, even in spite of the drink. The poet, you see, is lazy perforce; it's his job. Against his will, he has to stay still, like a fish in a pond. His particular struggle is the most difficult of all. He is completely caught, because his spirit must be perpetually *alight*. And his body suffers from the enforced rest. That's why, if you ask a poet to chop wood, he gets quite carried away after quarter of an hour. . . .

M.A.—But yoga is more than just a physical exercise. It's a philosophy.

L.D.—I don't give a damn about philosophy. I'm too stupid and I drink too much. I feel well in myself, on those occasions when I manage to dispel all thoughts of self. That sort of state of mind is the ideal springboard.

M.A.—But how do you reconcile that with your narcissism?

L.D.—I demand the right to contradict myself! As well as to use, and abuse, irony. The dichotomy of language is such that irony is the only authentic approach; it gives the other side, the obverse of the truth. If you take an idea apart you'll discover the ambivalence in it. By taking first one point of view and then the other you may occasionally light on the truth, but even then it slips through your fingers like water.

M.A.—It may surprise you when I say that this attitude is not unlike Montherlant's beloved 'alternance'.

L.D.—I have a great admiration for Henry de Montherlant. His work is a strange combination of the grotesque and the arid, but I find that sense of struggle lying at the heart of every sentence pleasing. And another thing, I can't picture him, his face escapes me. I've never met Graham Greene, for instance, or Jean-Paul Sartre, but I shouldn't be surprised if I were to go into a room and somebody said to me, 'This is Monsieur Sartre, or Mr Greene,' because I have a mental image of them. But Montherlant! As far as I'm concerned he belongs to the world of science fiction . . . a giant scorpion perhaps. I should be petrified to have to present myself to this monster as an ordinary two-legged human-being.

M.A.—I have seen him once or twice in the street in Paris, and I saw no sign of any antennae, prismatic eyes or forked tongues.

L.D.—He's a mulish Spaniard like Picasso, but one of the congealed, humourless ones.

M.A.—I don't agree. There are some irresistibly funny passages in Montherlant.

L.D.—Everything he touches turns to stone; he sets ideas in stone, and characters too and words. . . .

M.A.—That's the way volcanoes are!

L.D.—Perhaps basically that's where his merit lies. The man erects monuments. I must admit that if he were to come into the room this minute, I should be quite terrified. You might as well say, 'Aha! Here comes Dracula!'

He is a sort of Huysmans, only more controlled. I have a lot of respect for his way of pushing things to extremes. I always admire things I can't do myself. Montherlant deserves a bit of cherishing; he'll get it, mark my words, from the Left!

M.A.—And Camus?

L.D.—I have a soft spot for Camus. Like me he was a 'colonial'. He was the Beggar.

M.A.—And what's your attitude towards his work?

L.D.—I don't have attitudes. I have friendships and I have love. I try to make do with that.

M.A.—So how about Camus, then? Friendship or love?

L.D.—Love. I never knew him personally, so I can't talk as a friend or a witness. His weak point lay in the fact that he was French—French, excessively logical, like de Gaulle, and he didn't realize that that sort of thing wasn't fashionable any more. But a marvellous writer.

M.A.—People often talk about him as though he were a philosopher. Did he have a philosophy?

L.D.—No. And besides, you don't need a philosophy once you begin to understand what life can be—I don't mean what it is at this moment. Camus understood things that Sartre doesn't begin to grasp. Sartre doesn't instinctively see the obvious: he is always struggling to maintain his grip on it, and perhaps his greatness as a writer comes precisely from this effort, from this civil war between himself and things. But Camus' style has a serenity which enhances his language. Sartre is locked in everlasting combat. Unfortunately he has carried this conflict over into the purely ephemeral field of contemporary politics. In fifty years' time, you know, no one will give a damn about Cyprus, or Cuba, or the Greek colonels! Camus never really went in for that. He accepted his responsibilities as a citizen, but as a writer he always remained faithful to his art. He's a poet.

M.A.—They are both humanists.

L.D.—And both equally worthy from that point of view. It's their ways of shaping, of organizing reality, which differ. Sartre is a little like Bertrand Russell—for whom I have [*sic*] enormous respect: what chills me about them is that they think that it's possible to find a solution. You begin to live only when you have abandoned, rejected all solutions.

M.A.—A stoical approach, despair. . . .

L.D.—Not at all. It's joy. Despair has to be taken in the platonic sense: as an object in itself. It has nothing to do with being disappointed by the insurance company, or what have you.

M.A.—Alain Bosquet said to me, a few years ago now, talking about his friend, Cioran, the moralist: 'That's a man who has gone so far down into despair that he gives the impression of having found the key to happiness there. . . .'

L.D.—Yes, that's what I was trying to say: once the void has been recognized, defined, paced out, you have the beginnings of a sort of happiness. My answers are always so loose. . . .

M.A.—You make them loose deliberately because it's your way of answering or avoiding the question.

L.D.—No. It's my Irish clumsiness that does it. . . . The French are always after explanations, neat definitions for everything. It's absurd. Even when it's true it doesn't work. I'm an Irishman, and I speak English: you press the button and the music starts. The French language demands very concrete answers, perfectly expressed, to every problem, even the most insignificant. No poet can truly express himself except in his own language: only there does he have such a hair-trigger sense, an instinctive awareness of the direction in which it must all go. All the great comforts and joys of France come from a certain quality of restraint in the language. If you've got a guitar you can't expect to play it like a piano.

M.A.—Don't the nuances of different languages and different nations also correspond to differences in man?

L.D.—Man is the same everywhere.

M.A.—From a geographical point of view. But let's take it from the historical angle. There are several conceptions of man: classical man, purporting to be all of a piece, in harmony with a society which imagines itself universal.

L.D.—He doesn't exist.

M.A.—And there's contemporary man, who feels that he's a battlefield, split, torn apart inside by the confrontation of opposing forces.

L.D.—That's pure artistic invention. Men? I'll tell you what they're like: tall, medium or short; white, black, yellow or red, and whatever they are they have ears. The real problem is one of overpopulation; there are quite simply too many of us.

M.A.—But inside ourselves: solitude, duality, or is there a crowd there too?

L.D.—You put it in that typically French way which I so dislike. Very few human-beings could answer questions like that. I'm not a saint, neither am I Nietzsche: just something in between: a child, a poet, a drunken Irishman.

M.A.—What is an Irishman?

L.D.—A specialist in the manufacture and insertion of suppositories. We shove suppositories up the backsides of the English in London. A tough job, but so useful.

Elegy on Romanticism
and the Closing of
the French Brothels

M.A.—Have you noticed how rarely one meets a young poet these days who thinks of himself as an artist, or expects to be thought of as one? Today's poets are men in white coats with dissecting knives and computers. They don't *sing* any more, they carry out 'experiments in language'.

L.D.—I personally firmly believe in preserving the sense of *play*. I produce some frightfully serious nonsense. Too much self-control betrays a lack of application!

M.A.—Of course, in your private notebooks you do play with language; you shake it up quite vigorously, but you don't appear to want to ape a computer.

L.D.—A computer can produce texts of a kind, but its answers are no more than *data*: they rely entirely on programming. Whereas a poem provides answers to unasked questions.

M.A.—You have described the English language as a 'punching-ball'. Don't you agree that it lends itself better to this sort of experiment than French?

L.D.—By far, yes. Your syntax is so much less flexible. If you write bad French you end up with bad French. Whereas in English you can make any number of grammatical errors and still retain control, so that mistakes (whether or not they are deliberate) turn into gems. Take Conrad: his mistakes had such a beauty about them that the English ended by imitating them. A French poet needs a lot more temerity before he sets about destroying the grammar. When Rimbaud writes 'Je est un autre' he is deliberately attempting to break down logical structure; as a result he is thought of as a phenomenon. In England we take that sort of thing in our stride, as if the language belonged to each individual.

M.A.—How do you rate Rimbaud among the modern poets?

L.D.—He has taken all the glory because the surrealists adopted him as the forerunner of their own explorations. But I prefer Laforgue. Certainly Rimbaud is the greater poet, but Jules Laforgue didn't deserve to be so completely overshadowed by him. Perhaps it was the result of living abroad. There are very few French expatriates. They don't take well to exile, with the exception of Stendhal. The English, on the other hand, take to it remarkably well; wherever they go, they carry England with them. I love that absurd diplomat's life that Laforgue led. Like Nerval, he was deeply influenced by the German transcendentalists. And the way he married that English girl so that they could die together!

M.A.—The mystique of the English governess!

L.D.—I cannot understand why no major, definitive biography of Laforgue exists in French.

M.A.—That's easy. The C.N.R.S.* in France subsidizes only monographs on agriculture, herring fishing or com-

* Centre National de la Recherche Scientifique

parative studies of pig breeding in the Bas Languedoc and Basse Goulaine.

L.D.—A great shame.

M.A.—There's another thing. Laforgue was what can only be described as one of the 'weak heroes'. And the French like only 'strong heroes', even if they do come to bad ends.

L.D.—Pity the weak!

M.A.—And then too there is the problem of humour. The English take a positive view of humour. We don't; quite the opposite in fact. And Laforgue uses humour, like Charles Cros, another great poet: and the same thing happened to him.

L.D.—A poet needs to die young, if his life is going to match his work. It's absolutely useless to start off like Rimbaud and then end up an accountant at sixty. Those who go on and turn into peasants like Petrus Borel are pretty pathetic. . . . The whole thing takes on a rather theatrical quality.

M.A.—We demand a lot of poets, don't we?

L.D.—Certainly. We like everything to fit into a romantic pattern. If Dylan hadn't blown himself up with all that beer, if he were alive in London now, a hardened old soak who'd stopped writing, he'd have nothing like the same reputation.

M.A.—And there are some great artists who hide inside very introverted lives. Eliot is a case in point.

L.D.—Yes, there are poets who mature very late. Their reputations are less immediately brilliant, but often more lasting.

M.A.—We demand this fusion between the life and the work, but that isn't enough. The death, too, has to be right.

L.D.—You know, when I started off in my Greek islands, I was a sort of Gauguin. Then I went on and became the accountant-novelist. I've managed to trick fate.

M.A.—But doesn't the novel represent a sort of Harrar?

L.D.—You are so kind this morning! You keep guiding my steps along the most pleasing paths. Yes, perhaps the novel is an escape. I don't know.

M.A.—How do you stand as a poet in contemporary critical opinion?

L.D.—My success as a novelist has rather put me out of the running for the present. It's the principle of communicating vessels, you know: what you gain in one you lose in the other. Before the novels, I had an excellent reputation as a poet. No one pretended I was a genius, but I was among the six or seven good poets whose names would invariably be cited after the greats, Eliot, Auden, Dylan Thomas. I would often be somewhere in the next five. Two of my poems were included in the *Faber Book of Modern Verse* for twenty years. And then recently they decided that the anthology needed some new blood: five of us were shifted out to make room for five younger poets. So there you are. That's the position at the moment.

M.A.—I get the impression that you mind more about

what sort of reception your poems get than about your novels?

L.D.—Once one has published one's *Collected Poems*, one goes on being a poet, but one does so in a rather posthumous way. My four earlier volumes of selected poems have been put into one very fine book, which is doing well. I've gone on writing since then, but I haven't published anything outside reviews and magazines. If I live another ten years we'll be able to tell whether I'm finished or not, as the case may be. . . . Fashion enters into it too, you know, with poets. It changes all the time: sometimes one's in, sometimes not. And the name counts too, both ways. One must wait until the poems can be assessed on their own merits. I heard a story once about Paul Eluard. Apparently after the death of his mistress—

M.A.—His wife, Nusch.

L.D.—He decided to do away with 'Eluard' and he sent his new collection of poems round to publishers under a pseudonym. He used the name of a medieval monk or someone of the sort. It seems that no one wanted the manuscript and he was forced to revert to his own name.

M.A.—This must refer to *Le Temps déborde*, a marvellous collection that appeared in 1947 under the name of Didier Desroches. That same year Eluard published some erotic poems, *Corps mémorable*, under the name of Brun; they were dedicated to another woman. I suspect that the story of the refusals is a bit apocryphal. But it's true that Eluard had a great many imitators at that time!

L.D.—I don't care whether the story's true or not. There's a lot in it and I'm sticking to it.

M.A.—It certainly illustrates what you were saying about the importance of name and reputation. How many people in art galleries and museums look for the signature before even glancing at the picture?

L.D.—Look at Oscar Epfs! He owes everything to his name. . . .

M.A.—Another poet who featured in your life was Dylan Thomas, a man about whom we seem to know everything and yet nothing.

L.D.—He was a very shy man. That's why he drank. A terrific sensitivity. When he was alone with you he was kind, gentle, amusing, but as soon as he got into a crowd he would start swilling back the beer and in no time at all he would be drunk—he never was a really heavy drinker, he didn't have the head for it. Later on, when admirers began to gather round him, it got worse. He was dead scared of them. Apart from that he was an absolutely delightful companion.

The other day, Marc, I was looking at your handwriting and it struck me that it wasn't unlike Dylan Thomas's. I was reminded of something that happened once when I was working in the library at the British Museum. There was an exhibition of manuscripts on. I have an absolute passion for manuscripts, I find it thrilling to see the originals of great works. The library closed for lunch, so we had bought sandwiches and were wandering around the gallery. I had in my pocket a letter from Thomas, a poem that he had sent me for *The Booster*. Suddenly, in one of the cases I saw the same writing. 'It can't be,' I said, 'Dylan can't have made it here yet!' It was Emily Brontë. They were selling facsimiles of the manuscripts, so I bought the Emily Brontë and posted it to Dylan Thomas. He wrote back: 'Strange that fascimile by E. B. I thought it was a rejected poem of mine when I opened it. . . .' Later, in conversation, he added, 'But what's so strange about that? She's the only woman I've ever loved.'

M.A.—Very disturbing the way that handwriting moves through time like that. . . . In one very good piece you wrote on Thomas, you give a marvellous definition of his poetry: 'There are always trucks in his poems, running underground loaded with coal . . .'.

L.D.—I was trying to convey the colour of Wales which tinges all Dylan's poems. The thought-association is purely fortuitous. It happens that it touches on something fundamental.

M.A.—Dylan Thomas's position in English letters seems to have undergone a change in the last few years. After an extraordinary initial effervescence around the work and the man, there would appear to have been a slight falling off?

L.D.—Not really. In fact quite the reverse. His reputation is growing. He is as highly thought of as ever among the young, even if the critics talk less of him. All great poets who know how to limit their output win in the end. 'One mustn't write too much,' Dylan often used to say. He said it to me too, but then it's already too late. He left barely fifty poems, work of such richness that it still continues to glow, like a furnace, radiating heat and light. The one whose reputation has taken a downward turn is Auden, who used to be thought of as on a par with Eliot. Perhaps he too made the mistake of over-writing? But there again, one has to take account of fashion. No doubt time will put everything back in its rightful place.

123

M.A.—Thomas's work is spreading right across the world.

L.D.—Dylan is a problem as far as translation is concerned. There are some poets whose greatness lies not so much in what they have to say as in their language. Their metaphysic is worked out at the level of the interaction between the words. Dylan Thomas is like Mallarmé in that. In both of them the words matter more than the subject, which is often impossible to grasp. He's so dense, so allusive, so involved in the word, that you could never capture it in French. There are works like that. Similarly we'll never have in English *Les Moralités légendaires*. The transplant has been attempted five or six times, but it's not possible.

M.A.—The organism rejects the graft?

L.D.-Absolutely, like a foreign body.

M.A.—A difficult poet, but one who 'goes' well into French thanks to Pierre Leyris's admirable translation, is Gerard Manley Hopkins. And yet one might have thought that he too was untranslatable.

L.D.—It's not the same. With Hopkins, the problem is one of *rhythms*: with Thomas, it's *words*.

M.A.—Poets' poets, could one call them?

L.D.—Thomas could strike words like matches! He assembled sounds, structured silences, wove harmonies. He believed in hard work. Nothing made him more angry than to be accused of spontaneity. Until I saw him at work, I had imagined him rather like a volcano.

M.A.—I have seen some of Dylan's manuscripts: he

turned crossing-out into an art. . . . Before starting work he used to make endless lists of words.

L.D.—Yes, he was a volcano, but the lava was canalized in, and by, a method.

M.A.—You yourself are more elegiac, a solar poet.

L.D.—I have been heavily stamped by Greece, ancient and modern. It comes across in my poems. The trouble is that before you can understand me, you must first appreciate Greece. It means perhaps that I have over-localized my influences. Dylan always refused to go to Greece: he was afraid of anything that might take him away from himself.

M.A.—I can't help finding you too harsh in your assessment of your own poetry.

L.D.—I have produced five or six good poems. That's nothing to be ashamed of. I have tried always to be worthy of the light that shines in Greek metaphysics. Take Seferis's poems: they are painstakingly built up, word by word, but put them in the sun and they are transparent, seamless. I have merged with the Greeks like the Celts merged with the Visigoths in France.

M.A.—Your poetic language is always extremely precise. I would add that there is never any 'waste matter'. You've always published finished works, never rough drafts or sketches.

L.D.—I was lucky in having in T. S. Eliot an editor exceptionally lacking in indulgence. You cannot conceive how strict he was, rigorous almost to the point of cruelty. He read with total concentration, never letting anything slip, noting every weakness and pointing them out to one. 'I don't think such-and-such on page ten is worthy of you,' he used to say. I always followed his advice and whatever reputation I have for exactitude and rigorous precision comes purely from having had Eliot as a guide.

M.A.—Behind this apparent simplicity and innocence, your poetry is in fact a tight network of ideas and feelings.

L.D.—Yes. I've always tried to create pills.

M.A.—Capsules of reality?

L.D.—And of sensuality and intellectual acuity. I don't know whether the mixture is always perfect (or the dose), but if I have written even one poem that is fully successful in that way, it is this 'mixing' that is responsible. That is what produces the surface, at the same time strong and fragile, hermetic and luminous. The shell knitted to the body.

M.A.—How in fact do you write? Is it spontaneous or very controlled?

L.D.—I was a terrific word-hunter, an avid collector of images before the Eternal. But I was like Valéry when it came to the first line, 'the gift of the gods'. I would often have to wait ages for it. Whereas Dylan Thomas used to throw himself in and progress solidly word by word. Often I would have the idea, but it would be naked, no covering, no uniform for it. Dylan had a whole shopful of uniforms and the ideas used to take shape inside them. I could be brimming with ideas that I wanted to express, but still I had to wait for that something from outside, the necessary spark.

M.A.—I would say, from your work, that more often than not the outside event that sets off the poem is the awareness of the reality of a landscape, as though the space suddenly unfurled in your mind and started the words moving; like a mill-wheel when the water rushes into the race.

L.D.—You put it marvellously. Greek landscapes, particularly when I was young, had precisely that effect on me. They are, as it were, the co-authors of my poems.

M.A.—How about the Greek language?

L.D.—Modern spoken and written Greek is quite a recent creation. It is the product of a highly successful combination of Ancient Greek and other more simple languages. You can be standing talking to a peasant on the edge of a field and in one and the same sentence you'll hear two words that go right back to Plato, and two others coined in Constantinople in the last hundred years. It's an explosive mixture. Seferis always said the modern Greek is like those women who 'fart fire': hard to handle, but what delights! You can touch the reader with a word straight out of Socrates and at the same time you have a whole brand-new arsenal to hand: telephone, typewriter—all mod cons., what! It was a long, hard battle between the ancient and the modern; it was vital to dispel any artificiality: like Ireland, where everyone makes a great fuss about Gaelic just to annoy the Anglo-Irish. For a long time the Greeks were cursed with several different languages: one for the peasants, another for professors and journalists—not unlike China where there is a *written* language and a *spoken* language. Then the poets took up the cause of the purest of these languages, the demotic. And, after a bitter struggle, they won. The palette of modern Greek is enormously rich, very simple

127

and at the same time highly sophisticated in dealing with concrete and abstract alike.

M.A.—The fact that in this Babel-like maze it should have been the poets who brought about the triumph of the purest aspect of the language strikes me as an admirable vindication of their role and conclusive proof of their usefulness. It's worth bearing that in mind these days, when the value of poetry is so often questioned. Whenever a people senses that its language—i.e., its very soul—is threatened, it turns to its poets. The tragedy is that once the danger is past, the poets are completely forgotten.

L.D.—The purest of gifts offered to men who want nothing of them.

M.A.—Your poetry has something else in common with the Greek lyric, and that is an inclination towards the past. Your landscapes have an aura of history about them. The fruit and the light belong to the present, and yet they are the fruit and the light that have existed for centuries at the heart of that particular area.

L.D.—There is a point where sunlight and inner light meet. More especially when one is surrounded by monuments and relics and ruins. This mass of monuments is so boring, that just to escape the irritation one is tempted to revive them, to put some life into them.

M.A.—And so light collaborates with space.

L.D.—Yes. I have often found myself ringed by Roman ruins and I have to confess that while I appreciate the Roman attitude to landscape as well as their literature (Catullus, Propertius), I cannot take Roman landscape as a subject. I was steeped too young in the blue of Greece, which is both purer and more anarchic, subtleties that correspond more closely with my own sensitivity.

M.A.—Talking of the Romans, Joyce once said something like, 'What kind of men were they? The minute they arrived in a country, the first thing they thought about was digging drains!'

L.D.—I sympathize with that. The Romans were very like the British. For a sensualist hot baths and drains are very important. It was the Egyptians who invented the flush lavatory, a fantastic advance. So you see I'm not *that* against civilization. Look what's going on in Nigeria, in India. . . . The English may have been stupid and unimaginative, but they did construct solid frameworks in their colonies, like the Romans. I'm for the triumph of nationalism, but not when it means unleashing *on a permanent basis* all the most savage instincts. Besides, you often find among newly-independent peoples a sort of nostalgia for the old colonialists. In India, for instance, the ruling classes are going back to an English way of life, starting clubs etc.

M.A.—I don't much like the Romans, myself, probably on account of their efficiency, but one can't deny that their type of civilization is the complement of the Greek.

L.D.—It's thanks to the Romans that we know the Greeks. And one musn't forget that the Romans did have a sense of pleasure.

M.A.—Thank you. You've given me the link I was looking for. I was wondering how to get from the Romans to a poem of yours called 'Elegy on the Closing of the French Brothels'.

L.D.—A Roman orgy is as good a way as any.

M.A.—Usually your poetry is about 'noble' subjects. But there is an element of humour, too, and it seems to me that when it comes to the point the scandalous nature of this poem represents a sane reaction. If one sees everyday language directed at the sublime as an overdrawn bow-string, wouldn't you agree that one finds in the 'Elegy' a way of unbending the bow?

L.D.—It's a very serious subject. The French brothel was the equivalent of the English pub, more a meeting-place than a pleasure palace. There was nothing dirty or shady or sinister about it. It was an important centre of French social life. Sociologically the brothel was an excellent institution, hospitable and necessary. When I wrote the line, 'All the great brothels closed save Sacré-Cœur', it was aimed at English puritanism. There was an element of irony, of course, but it was a subject that fully deserved to be written about. The 'maisons closes' provided the settings for some marvellous encounters; that was where I met all the Anglo-American poets. I spent some fabulous hours with Henry Miller at the Sphinx in Montparnasse.

M.A.—But why French brothels in particular? I should have thought they existed everywhere.

L.D.—Neither in Greece nor in England. There were 'clandés', 'maisons de tolérance', where the atmosphere was really unsavoury, but nothing like the French brothels, where you could go just for a chat or a drink. I found the French lack of hypocrisy towards an institution that everywhere else was viewed with horror most sympathetic. Sexually I've always been rather modest and always in love with someone, which doesn't give one a taste for going to brothels as a 'consumer'. But I had a friend who absolutely adored whores: he would take a taxi and say, 'Straight to the nearest brothel, quick as you can!' When he came back to France after the war, he got in a taxi in Marseilles and gave his usual direction. 'Ah, Monsieur,' the taxi-driver said mournfully, 'The brothels are all closed. Pleasure is dead!'

M.A.—What is the connection with religion, since you stress that aspect in the poem.

L.D.—A lot of Frenchmen were convinced that the Church owned and ran brothels on the side. I don't know how much truth there was in that. But isn't the Church after all the great emotional brothel? In Montparnasse everyone believed that the Sacré-Cœur would never have been as big without the contributions from the brothels.

Tunc, Nunquam:
The Struggle for Happiness

M.A.—Recently you returned to the novel with an enormous work in two volumes, *Tunc* and *Nunquam.* Why the Latin titles?

L.D.—What I wanted was to establish right from the start the two time-scales of the narrative: *then,* which suggests the distortion of the imaginary, and *now,* which opens the way to reality. Questions on one side, answers on the other. I was determined to involve the reader in the circuit, to get him out of his passive role as onlooker by making him the subject of the novel in the second volume, one of the characters.

M.A.—Indeed, I get the impression that *Nunquam* is a snare. *Tunc* captivates but *Nunquam* captures!

L.D.—I don't know whether I succeeded, but I conceived the book as a reader-trap! The story is the bait, then the trap springs shut.

M.A.—And it's the reader's turn to be read!

L.D.—Yes, if the mechanism has worked properly.

M.A.—Do you think it's possible to summarize in a few words the subject of this highly involved novel, which seems to spread in so many different directions?

L.D.—I got the inspiration for it from Spengler's famous book *The Decline of the West*, which contained some astonishing foresights, including Cæsarism (which culminated in nazism) and gold, a notion which heralded Freud's theories. It is the story of a young inventor who needs society in order to implement his discoveries. Every invention has a universal significance. I also use it to make a few predictions of my own. It's all absurd, crazy—in other words, accurate.

M.A.—There's more than one allusion to *The Black Book* in this latest novel. What's one to make of that? Is it intended as a parody, or does it reveal a desire to conclude a much earlier part of your work?

L.D.—Oh! I simply enjoy making little links like that, that's all. My ideas haven't changed that much.

M.A.—What's the underlying meaning of the work? At times one seems to see a fierce critique of culture.

L.D.—The idea is that it's impossible to escape from civilization. Culture is another matter: a bad conscience, which has no effect on reality. One has the right to ask questions, but no one can answer, except for himself. My character (who is the opposite of a poet: a wild plant, a thistle) invents while others question themselves or knock their heads against brick walls. Basically there's nothing original in the book. Everything is pinched! Except the way the ideas are set out.

M.A.—There's a different tone about the writing of *Tunc*, quite unlike the *Quartet*: an ironic, caustic, irrepressible zest.

L.D.—Certainly there's a change in technique. I decided to do away with the descriptions of landscape, the set pieces, the purple passages, etc. In the *Quartet* they were all essential if the reader were to get through four volumes. Here irony starts to show its face. I am getting closer to Poe. I tell you what it is: it's Pursewarden's 'tone'.

M.A.—I really like what you say about *Tunc*: '*Tunc* does not pretend to pretend. All the characters are as real as you or me; and in the end they die happy like all readers and all writers . . .'. But this too reveals the new caustic attitude of mind (a despair breaking into peals of laughter) that I talked of earlier. Do you despair?

L.D.—Yes, but happily so. It makes me think of Stendhal's last words, 'Farewell, but be cheerful about what happens.'

M.A.—Why?

L.D.—Without despair we should have no conception of joy.

M.A.—What can one do when one finds oneself in such a frame of mind?

L.D.—One turns it into farce, into happiness.

M.A.—Who was the most desperate man you've met in your life?

L.D.—A millionaire!

M.A.—How is this kind of anxiety revealed in *Tunc* and *Nunquam*?

L.D.—The confrontation between inner riches and worldly riches. It's the struggle for happiness.

M.A.—Would you say that your friend Dylan Thomas, whose death in New York was tantamount to suicide from an overdose of alcohol and Americans, was a desperate man?

L.D.—Dylan was an alcoholic, but there was more joy in his soul than there was whisky in his liver. . . . He succumbed to his feeling of panic in the face of the work still to be done. A perfect example of rejection.

M.A.—A terrible, untimely death. . . .

L.D.—Great men always choose the right moment at which to die, when everything is ready for their exit.

M.A.—What are your plans for the future?

L.D.—I am tempted to give the same answer as Blanco, the tramp. 'Plans? Me, monsieur?' In fact I'm waiting for the proofs of a little book, a sort of notebook: notes on Blood, Psyche, material. Then I'm thinking of publishing the poems that I've written in the last three years. As for novels, we'll have to wait and see.

M.A.—One sometimes gets the impression that you find literature a burden, that your books, written or waiting to be written, encircle you like prison walls.

L.D.—One should never start writing. If only I'd known. . . .

M.A.—If you had to sum up briefly the meaning of your life and of your work, what would you say?

L.D.—I should reply like Talleyrand: 'And above all, monsieur, not too much zeal!'

138

Les Suppositoires Requisitoires

Lawrence Durrell

The dawn of that New Age was dated from the moment when the first book of poems by a defective and visionary computer was launched upon an astonished world; poems far denser and far richer than the greatest work of the past. Thus the new age was marked by the emergence of a new root-race named the Cogitergs in memory of Descartes. Their God was named Mobego. The displacement and overthrow of the vampiric culture of Jesus was at hand. He had thrown his plasm-hunger across the span of a thousand years and more, just as a ventriloquist throws his voice. Symbolized by the cannibal sacrament, he had established the pedigree of the chosen race, the poets, whom Plato had tried in vain to expel. In the great churches they are still drinking by blood-group. It is thicker than water, more inebriating than wine. In the clutch of this vampire's dream all history was paralysed. The dream was of blood, the blood-stained faeces of the martyrs. The cult of the dead vampire was pre-eminent; it began with the crucifixion—for that was the common fate of the vampire in classical times. The symbolism of the Event is clearly read—the crown of thorns, the stake through the side. Thus with the coming of the Cogitergs our poetic pedigree was revealed for what it was—the word in all its dichotomy. In the beginning was the word, and the word was Blood. But now it gives way to the richer, more constant, but sexless number. (Fear, that highly dependable emotion, is still there, but its sources change. No longer a fear that the vampire will rise and walk unless propitiated by a sacrament of blood. Fear rather that a defective computer might vote itself into supreme power. A computer with a number-neurosis.) This is what they tell us. The metaphor parading in its underclothes. Take up thy bed and walk. Give us this day our daily brood.

> Yes but...
> But nothing.
> Probability
> Plausibility.
> What are you saying my friend?

Concrete poem and Lettrist jingle are pathetic attempts to propitiate the new God. Man now tries to *imitate* the computer. Genuflections to the mechanical lapsus. But wait. Suppose a computer fell in love with a man, tried to imitate him? Would not that argue a neurosis?

SUPPOSE, SUPPOSE, SUPPOSITOIRE

The psi experience in science is psiritual.

What sort of a product is a culture in your opinion? It is a product of tensions, stresses which cannot be relieved in any other way. The stresses rise from the infantile complexes of man. A culture is a safety valve against impulses we dare not admit into the arena of full consciousness because they imperil our reason and deform the godlike image we have of ourselves; our rational desires, our hunger for order and calm, which we know to be the only fruitful factors in physical or psiritual growth are perpetually thrown into disarray by the uprush of the death-forces from the unconscious. We are ruled by this spirit of contradiction; our reason attempts to put a good face on the truth, our wickedness wears a saintly mask. But at every remove our bloodthirsty sadism jumps the rails, jumps the gun. Civilization proceeds steadily through rape murder pillage, and nothing can contain these impulses, not even magics like religion, rituals like prayer or football, or the substitution of ritual blood for the real stuff we long to drink (alcohol).

The basic dichotomy between unconscious impulses (our rulers) and conscious desires is reflected in the structure of language. Words are bifurcate, double-dealing.

The basic fear which drives us towards an insight into ourselves or an enquiry into the world around us is death; the irreversibility of process, the lunge towards dissolution, towards rotting and melting.

Landscape invents language and language poets.
Ursa Major and Ursa Minor should not be confused.
The man-cocoon is this thing
Tool-bearing
Tale-telling
Childbearing
Agribronzocultivated
Vegetocarnivorefacient....

The Sarcophagus ends all—the flesh-eater, the death-munching coffin, darkness-propelled.

How well we know the piety of the killers.
The Romans were siezed by the same convulsion.
Our turn has come.

In the red lingo blood is king, red uniforms for wars, red rags for bulls, bloodstock thicker than waters, white feathers for the men without red blood, bled white—the jews have no word for gentiles treated kosher as to blood...
Bloodstock.
Blue-blood (arterial rather than veinous), the top sign of kings.

In the Chinese style of divination as exemplified by the Books of Changes we are shown how to manipulate the inevitable.

The marvellous thing is that nature is an adventurer and quite empirical. She is self-taught. Anything could happen. The whole of process renews itself with every heart-beat.

So process is a self-perpetuating act of insight on the part of the universe as a whole.

S. indignantly abandoned his mathematical studies as soon as he discovered what he took to be their basic dishonesty; namely that if two minus quantities are multiplied the answer is a plus.

> We must speak today
> In private parentheses
> Or personal puns,
> Poems like expiring suns.

A world forgetting how to read—renouncing the personal adventure to the interior where the big intuitions lie waiting to be verified. In favour of a communal throb in which the image will displace the numinous personal symbol.

Twenty-four frames a second is the camera-speed of the modern consciousness—of reality filtered through light on to celluloid. The older arts also used time and causality but the intention was different—it was a mind-stilling operation. But the mechanism of the camera militates against this end: perpetually on the move, destroying and dispersing the still centre of concentration, flooding the eye of the mind with a flow of sensation. The consciousness with its flux of disorderly sensations which the Indians sought to halt and refine; in virtues of these practices that restless thing called Mind, so hard to control because of its inability to function apart from the breathing process, is disciplined, freed from its dependence on breath.

Such serial images flatter the root cause of our unease, our anxiety, and strengthen the hold of the ego by dispersing attention.

Once an organism learns to think, it loses the ability to regenerate an amputated limb.

It is interesting to note that the human extremities are of the primitive quinquifid type, long since superseded in most of the higher vertebrates. The human hand displays a very early phylogenetic form similar to that found in some lower vertebrates as well as in the dragons of pre-history.

We shall be compelled to talk
                    only
In puns so that our children
                    computers
                        should not understand

The Sphinx; incontinence or the relaxation of the sphincters: prophecy!

> Seek seek
> Hide hide
> Cheat cheat
> Spoil spoil

> Narcissistic lovers
> Were they born in couples
> Paired and unpaired
> Pure or impure?

> The unbearable
> is forgetting

Furthermore, according to modern anthropological teaching, almost all those physical characteristics that are specifically human betray the perpetuation of embryonic features which, among the higher vertebrates, undergo profound changes during the period of gestation. Without going into detail, it is sufficient to note that orthognatism in the human adult, his lack of pelt, the inadequate pigmentation of his skin, the central position of the fontanel, the disproportionate weight of his brain, the persistence of the cranial sutures, the retention of a fine, unpigmented down, as well as his S-shaped spine, are all features of an embryonic state which disappear in the higher vertebrates prior to birth or in very early infancy and develop into specialized structures. This primitivism is not only characteristic of the fully formed adult body, it is also evident in the embryo from the earliest stages.

And so man freed himself from Nature and became his own creator, he made his own organs, became man the 'tool-maker', the 'tool-making animal'. The animal is a slave to his organs, man is master of his tools.

Brave words; but at what point does he become the victim of the phantom hand, the spade?

The pen is mightier than the spade, would you say? Both are phantom extensions of the mind.

Work was the earliest tranquillizer against anxiety, and will always remain the best.

Primitive men, in a similar situation, react quite differently. The vision that we would call hallucinatory and false, seems to them on the contrary privileged.

It takes the mysterious dynamism of madness, the primitivism of the child to build the archaic of modern materials.

The traditional country advice to anyone looking a bit under the weather, 'go and get yourself a drink at the slaughterhouse', was taken up in the city by 'fin de siècle' Paris society who, after a night of excess, would go to the La Villette slaughterhouses for a 'pick-me-up'.

Ailing Roman patricians used to go down into the arena to slake their thirst on the losing gladiators, while in Germany, before the First World War, epileptics were treated with the still warm blood to be found at places of execution in the early morning.

Blood can restore an invalid to health. The first transfusion, prescribed by a Jewish doctor, cost the lives of three young men for the temporary recovery of Pope Innocent VIII.

Since perfected and no longer so dramatic, transfusion is nowadays practised widely and successfully, appreciated by the donors even more than by the receivers.

There is never a shortage of willing blood donors, even when they are not urgently nèeded.

Among some semitically influenced African tribes, the labia majora of three-year-old girls are sewn together. The only person allowed to reopen them will be their husband, who will have to use a knife.

Des pièces engagées? non! plutôt des pièces détachées

DATA

Heartbeat 70 per minute
The human cell contains 23 pairs of chromosomes
21,600 breaths a day
900 an hour or 15 each minute

In fact it's literature RATHER
That bores me IN LIFE
I prefer, dear,
Snow, cars, women
More demanding preferences by far
No excessively determined structures
Far less predictable emotions
    Incorruptible
    Suppositions
Women, cars, snow,
(Melon, strawberry, apple)
Yes, it's literature that bores me
Ah! a car makes one feel so good!
A woman so deliciously anxious!
Snow refreshes in an instant
Snow on one's neck
But, the ultimate joy of
All
Three at once—*WHEEEEEE*
Indeed *VROOM VROOM GDOING*
    it is
Literature that bores me

A lion, he was thrown to the Christians

EPITAPH ON THE TOMB OF THE VAMPIRE POET
'Too much self-control betrays a lack of application'

Madness is the forgery of true experience

Life and 'Method' in the mathematical sense are made of the same stuff. If you interfere with the purity of function you bring about the death of species. It is our case. *Homo sapiens moriturus...*

VIVE DURRELL, FARCE DE LA NATURE!

When Faust spoke the forbidden wish 'Verweile doch, du bist so schon' (Moment, stay now! You are so beautiful), the Devil came and took his soul.

In the genetic make-up of things lies the 'signature' of their ultimate form. In the genes of man lies something which will mysteriously unfold into nose, lip, eyebrow, hand. Everything begins 'in potentia' and gradually actualizes. Meanwhile, at every stage everything is changing into everything else. When a man sharpens his intuition enough, becomes enough of a poet, he can read the signature inherent in things and in people; he can reach behind appearances to divine their ultimate form. He reaches the Heraldic Reality where art has its roots.

Those whose task it was to investigate the hidden powers, the laws and sympathies of nature were called *Physiki* of the daimonian order which stands between men and the Gods. (Plato)

Poetry, like life itself, is far too serious not to be taken lightly.

Astrological Portrait of Lawrence Durrell

by Conrad Moricand

Moricand based this astrological horoscope on a date
provided by his friend Henry Miller. He was not to
meet Durrell till years later. Moricand was the
central character in Henry Miller's book *The Devil
in Paradise*.

The subject of this portrait is a highly complex one, who deceives both himself and those around him as to his true nature; everything about him that appears good is in fact bad, and vice versa: everything which could be bad is excellent. This comes from Jupiter being the ruling planet in this horoscope, not only in the East—where it is in close conjunction with the ascendant in Sagittarius—but also in the III House in Pisces where it influences the Sun and Mercury. Jupiter is the great bringer of good fortune and change. Jupiter always helps the subject fall on his feet, regardless of the vicissitudes of fate.

The subject in question is a pure intellectual, with a highly developed critical and analytical sense—the Sun as the ruling planet being in conjunction with Mercury in the III House—so that he is in a position to make use of the fundamental contradictions in his nature for his work. But the contradictions are none the less there, deep down, in spite of all appearances.

This overall picture, a somewhat unusual one, is created by the perilous position of Jupiter, in close conjunction with the ascendant in Sagittarius, its domicile, where it is in an unremittingly bad position in opposition to Mars and in square with the Sun. The Sun in conjunction with Mercury is partially responsible for this malefice, being in Pisces, the second house of Jupiter, and furthermore in a square with Mars and with the ascendant. The result of this is that Jupiter, the beneficient planet *par excellence*, the 'fix anything' planet, features in a rather bad position in this horoscope, which is almost entirely dominated by him. This means that the subject will need to call on all the vast resources of his mind in order to maintain a balance.

The mind here is in part indicated by the triplicity of air, which is the most important element here, marking the subject with its imprint and ultimately proving of great assistance. So the intellect comes first and then on the intuitive level: adaptability, flexibility and taste.

The nature of air is subtle and invisible, asserting itself only when compressed. Air is living and pure, or polluted. Air generates the gently rocking breeze and the rending storm. Air created speech; its voice is soft or terrifying. Air kindles the fire and feeds the flames. In the presence of air, water dries out, turns to dust. Air, ruling over the breathing of all things, presents the character of spiritual nourishment.

The subject's way of behaving in society is indicated by Sagittarius rising at 6°, in conjunction with Jupiter, one of the ruling planets.

The sign of Sagittarius is represented as 'a musketeer, looter of works of art, on a galloping horse', which indicates religious feelings in a rebellious heart. There is a dual symbolism: the human torso suggests respect for established law and order, while the horse's body and hooves indicate the rebelliousness of the wild animal.

Sagittarius produces a fiery character, with a taste for danger and competition for the race which must be won, and an optimistic approach to all trials and tribulations.

The aspect is a laughing, cheerful one; a great deal of zest and self-assurance. The subject is courteous, gentle and attractive; his voice is clear and vibrant; *he draws people to him with words*. Always on the alert, he makes decisions quickly and good-humouredly. He is always on the lookout to see what effect he is making, more concerned about his status than about his worth. His principle concern is 'to sugar the pill' for himself and for others.

He delights in risks and recklessness, which is an attractive characteristic; and intrigue, which is less so. He enjoys setting traps.

This is a two-sided character, reserved and difficult to get to know. He demonstrates, always, a certain *reserve*, as much towards himself as towards others. His manner is likeable, often becoming abrupt and wary for fear of 'what people will say'.

Silent at times, irrepressible at others. An apparent weakness of character, then, suddenly, boldness and even violence. The subject is capable of being carried away by enthusiasms, and liable to self-delusion at every turn. He is very susceptible to mirages. Above all, a delight in paradox and lost causes; he defends them all chivalrously and most loyally. Strength here resides in a sense of ease.

Sagittarius, however, gives us only the outer man; the Sun in conjunction with Mercury in Pisces will show us how to get behind the appearances and approach the deeper nature.

The sign of Pisces is 'an angel surrounded by flames', which indicates love of spirituality in the midst of obstacles of all kinds. Pisceans vary enormously according to the lives that they lead. Sometimes it is the sign of universal love and initiation, sometimes of vital error and indifference. There is a systematic search for the ideal, but which remains sometimes 'beside the point'. Pisceans are always at the extremes of Good or Evil.

Pisces gives rise to a passive nature, 'malleable', highly impressionable, whose personality exists mainly in relation to others. The psychological mimicry of the Piscean places the subject in an imaginary life, which is, *par excellence*, that of the actor, where the lack of a precise character forces him almost always to be playing a part.

It is therefore curious to recall here that on the mythological and symbolic plane of correspondences, Jupiter, master of Pisces and of the ascendant, symbolizes the vital cosmic fluid, which sustains man's vital principle. It is because of this very subtle essence that he is known as the 'root of the sea' and that his weapon is thunder. He penetrates all things. He is the 'protean' god of a thousand metamorphoses, who assumes all shapes to impregnate all goddesses. He is at the same time the essence of fire, the father of men and gods, and the life-breath of all beings.

The Sun in conjunction with Mercury in Pisces is also in square with Jupiter and Mars, which seriously hinders the potential of the temperament and of the faculties. On one side it exaggerates the subject's malleability, which exposes him to too many influences over which he has no control; on the other it gives him a rather aggressive critical attitude, justified no doubt by this exceptional malleability. One possible result is a state of disorder and anarchy in the mind and in the emotions, which could lead to the sterilization or corruption of the faculties through encouraging the subject to spread himself across too many areas, and often in vain quests.

This natural disposition is reinforced by the aspect of the VII House, which refers not only to marriage and all unions, but also to the subject's contacts with society. Mars on the cusp of the VII House, and the Moon, isolated, are once more conjoined, not very harmoniously, combining a state of total emotional dependence with an acutely competitive sense. Consequently the subject is always finding himself on the defensive, adopting a permanently 'critical' attitude, which is further indicated by the highly important role played by Uranus in conjunction with Venus in her domicile, Aquarius, so emphasizing the erotic side and the total nonconformism of the character. All those who, like the subject, are ruled by this planet, live in a constant state of revolt, always suffering because of their ties and their limitations, because of the frameworks within which they must evolve if they are to continue living.

And so we come to what is best in this horoscope, by which I mean the conjunction of Venus and Uranus in Aquarius, which, reinforced by the excellent aspects of Saturn in Taurus and Neptune in Cancer, indicates not only a deeply intuitive sense but also an almost 'musical' freedom of movement within knowledge. The protean side of Jupiter opens the door to all the spheres of the mind, even the most subtle, and to all the heavens of knowledge, overlapping one another like the 'Great Terrestrial and Divine Onion' of the Cabbala. Thanks to Uranus the mind is transformed into a *rocket*, a brilliant antenna, the only serious risk being that it might lose itself by abandoning all contact with earth. For there are three kinds of thought: the head, the chest and the stomach, which is the best, because it symbolizes the Earth, but it is not the one preferred by the subject. All strong work must be rooted in the Earth, otherwise it risks being toppled by Jupiter from the higher regions of the heavens, like Vulcan, who was lame for ever after as a result.

A horoscope of great style, which goes somewhat beyond the subject in the extent of the area which he is capable of exploring, but which remains none the less the most beautiful of all 'Invitations to the Voyage.'